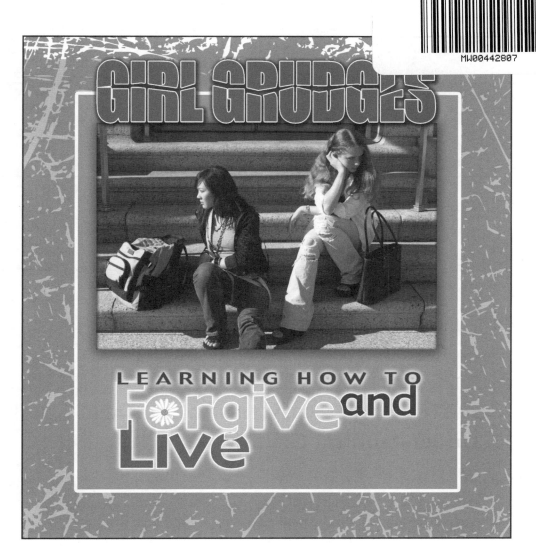

© 2007 by YouthLight, Inc.
Chapin, SC 29036

Cover Design and Layout by Diane Florence
Special Graphic Assistance by Amy Rule
Project Editing by Susan Bowman

ISBN: 1-59850-033-3

EAN: 978-1-59850-033-2

Library of Congress Number
2007930090

10 9 8 7 6 5 4 3 2 1
Printed in the United States

Table Of
CONTENTS

SECTION THREE: Integrate

SECTION THREE: ACTIVITIES TO INTEGRATE
Interventions to Integrate Change

Acknowledgements

We wish to recognize the many girls who shaped the content of this book. Our interactions with them showed us how serious the impact of a grudge can be, as well as how possible it is to "forgive and live." In light of the recent loss of lives at both Virginia Tech University and the Amish Nickel Mines School, we salute Youthlight for taking a proactive step to address the safety of youth in neighborhoods, schools, and colleges. Those researchers who have devoted their lives to understanding forgiveness also helped us fit the pieces of this book together. Lastly, within our own faith traditions, we have found the essential truths of living peacefully with others.

Dedication

We dedicate Girl Grudges to: girls who will be part of the activities in this book, those who have lost their lives because of a grudge, and to our families for their love and support.

About the Authors

Cheryl Dellasega, PhD is a Professor of Humanities at Penn State University, College of Medicine, and Professor of Women's Studies, Penn State University. She is also the award winning author of five books on female relationship issues: *Surviving Ophelia* (Perseus, 2001; Ballentine, 2003), *Girl Wars* (with Charisse Nixon) (Fireside, 2004), *The Starving Family* (Champion Press, 2005), *Mean Girls Grown Up* (Wiley, 2005), and *Forced to be Family* (Wiley, 2007). Her first novel in a young adult series titled "Bloggrls" is *Sadie:Nugrl90* (Marshall Cavendish, 2007). Dr. Dellasega is recognized internationally as an expert on adolescent girls. Club and Camp Ophelia, two programs she founded, have helped thousands of teens learn the important lifeskill of creating and maintaining positive relationships with peers.

Shileste Overton Morris, is the Youth Development Program Manager at the Center for Schools and Communities. Her expertise is in training youth workers in areas specific to cultural and social competency, pregnant and parenting teens, afterschool programming and other youth development related topics. She is currently a Fellow at the Institute for Educational Leadership based in Washington, D.C. Ms. Overton-Morris has collaborated with Dr. Dellasega on many Club and Camp Ophelia programs and trainings.

Together, Dr. Dellasega and Ms. Overton-Morris have founded It Takes a Girl, Inc., an organization dedicated to the belief that "It Takes a Girl to Change the World." Our work helps adolescents and adults achieve that goal, one relationship at a time.

Introduction

Grudges are a common problem for girls, particularly during the middle school years when relationally aggressive or female-type bullying behaviors peak. This book is written for teachers, counselors, and others who care about girls and want to help them change their relationships from poisonous to positive. A combination of clinical perspectives, scholarly insights, and experiential strategies are provided for use with girls alone or in groups across a variety of settings. The goals of this book are to:

- Educate readers about the grudge dynamic and behaviors associated with it
- Relate the impact of grudges to oneself and others
- Integrate new knowledge to create interventions which can change grudge-related behaviors

Each goal is addressed in a separate section of the book, and activities follow which are structured to compliment the text.

How to Use This Book

This book is designed for use in many different ways. An individual therapist or counselor can choose to read through the contents and select specific activities with clients in one-to-one or group settings. Teachers might choose to use some of the material for a single unit on grudges or incorporate activities as an ongoing program. Other adults might choose to sit down with one or more girls and work through the book in stages from beginning to end. Throughout, we have changed specific identities and names to protect those girls who might otherwise be recognized.

The model used to develop this guide was developed by Dellasega (2002). Abbreviated as E-R-I or Educate-Relate-Integrate, this conceptual framework has been used in Club and Camp Ophelia™ as well as other educational venues where the goal is behavior change.

Educate is the process of creating a framework of understanding that will help learners appreciate the basic facts about a topic, which in this case is girl grudges. **Relate** refers to the practice of self assessment, where girls apply new knowledge to their personal situations. **Integrate**, the final phase, involves assimilating new skills and behaviors, and creating a plan for change.

Section One
EDUCATE

Definitions

Merriman-Webster Dictionary Merriam-Webster, (2005) defines a grudge as: "A feeling of ill will or resentment," while the Random House *Webster's Unabridged Dictionary* (2005) says: "A grudge is a feeling of resentment harbored because of some real or fancied wrong." The latter source identifies bitterness, rancor, malevolence, enmity, and hatred as synonyms for a grudge. Regardless of how you define a grudge, there's no doubt about the impact of these unyielding conflicts. Here's what some girls have to say:

Corrie, age 14:

"A grudge is like prejudice, only against a person instead of a group. It is holding on to something that happened in the past and was long over." She admits to holding grudges, particularly one time when a friend cancelled coming to her birthday party at the last minute. This led to a lack of trust for several years, and even now, they are not as close although Corrie recognizes that she needs to let go of her feelings and move on. She says girls need to stop caring about what caused the grudge, and points out that often the person you're holding a grudge against doesn't even know how you feel. She thinks grudges in girls run deeper than for boys, and that boys can often make up and walk away from conflict in a way girls can't.

Imani, age 15:

"A grudge is holding resentment toward someone because of something they did to me." She describes a situation where one girl "stole" another girl's boyfriend, which led to an ongoing grudge, and believes we all need to apologize more, even when we think we're right. It's also important to communicate better the FIRST time you are hurt.

Josey, age 11:

"A grudge is a fight that someone has held for a long time." She gives the example of a friend who thought she was annoying and would always call her names. Her advice is for girls to just forgive each other, to think about fights for a little bit of time but then let them go. She says boys don't get into grudges as much—they beat each other up and then walk away.

Saleena, age 15:

"A grudge is a type of anger you keep inside for a long time." She gives an example of a situation where a girl was excluded from the birthday party of her best friend, which precipitated a grudge. Her advice? Try to understand that mistakes can be made on both sides, and come to an agreement, not in a mean way. She says girl grudges tend to last longer and are mostly for unimportant reasons.

Although it might seem that the grudge mindset would be outgrown, even grown adult women have strong feelings about grudges, as illustrated by the following comments:

J.P., a 30-something hair stylist:
"Women are definite grudge holders, more than men. As a hairstylist I hear many stories from women about why they don't like someone because of something that happened a long time ago. It might be over a boyfriend, or another incident that they don't even care about anymore, but they still don't like the person."

A.W., 40, mom of four:
"Women typically have a harder time letting things go, they remember everything and don't have a problem reminding you, if you forget. One of my friends is a big grudge holder, especially when it comes to her marriage. She remembers every mistake her husband ever committed, and reminds him about it every chance she gets. She just won't get over it. She doesn't see how it is affecting their relationship in an unhealthy way."

L.T., a female Administrative Assistant:
"Grudges take on a life of their own, they can become so out of control. I think most people let their emotions take over, so much so, they forget what the initial grudge was even about."

K.P., 36, Manager:
"It's easier to hold a grudge towards someone than tell them they hurt your feelings. If the hurt is not acknowledged, then your feelings cannot be validated, only internalized. At work, you can really see grudges in action between women who are mad at each other because something was misunderstood or miscommunicated. Then those feelings turn to resentment and make it very hard to get work accomplished. Sarcasm and exclusion are two big ways I see grudges played out."

Working Definition
For the purpose of this book, our definition of a grudge is:

"Sustained negative perceptions about one or more persons (or events associated with them), leading to ongoing negative thoughts and/or behaviors."

Throughout this book, we will refer to the begrudger as the girl who initiates the grudge and the begrudged as the target of her hostility, although we recognize that there are many situations where both girls are equally resentful and invested in maintaining the grudge. We also believe that many other girls beyond those immediately involved in the conflict are deeply impacted by the situation.

Examples

In the media, there are subtle messages that can make holding grudges seem glamorous. The movie *Bring It On* (Reed & Bendinger, 2000), geared for a teen girl audience and so popular it earned a sequel, features an ongoing grudge between cheerleaders in two distinctly different high schools. Television shows such as *America's Next Top Model* (Jenkins, 2003) and *My Super Sweet Sixteen* (Juan & Chang, 2005) portray women and girls as ever ready grudge holders, with the implicit endorsement of a grudge as completely normal. Teen reads such as *The Clique Series* (Harrison, 2006) and *Gossip Girls* (Ziegesar, 2003) have taken grudge holding to an art form. These books, read by teens and adults alike, are focused on gossiping, manipulating and backstabbing, making the bad girl look good, or at least making the reader feel a love/hate relationship with the characters. Even fairy tales often have a female grudge at the heart of the story. Consider:

- Cinderella's stepsisters disliked her because she was the blood daughter of their father
- Sleeping Beauty was put to sleep by an "old fairy" who had a longstanding grudge against the royal kingdom
- Snow White was envied by her stepmother, who continuously checked to make sure her stepdaughter's beauty hadn't surpassed her own

Gender Differences

We believe girl grudges are different from boy grudges in many ways because of the special meaning relationships hold for girls. Specifically, they are:

Denial

Egocentric

Emotional

Persistent

Denial occurs because of a failure to recognize that it takes two parties to keep a grudge going. Often, the begrudger doesn't recognize her own role in creating and maintaining a grudge, and may even feel her hostility is deserved.

Egocentric refers to the self centeredness of grudges. Often there is a sense of indignity, anger, and resentment within the begrudger that perpetuates the grudge. Within a girl's mind, the grudge can take on bigger than life proportions and become all important, even if no one else knows it exists.

Emotional means that grudges often arise from feelings rather than fact. For girls, emotional wounds are often deeper than physical wounds, and can continue to hurt long after the initial insult or misunderstanding occurred.

Persistent describes the nature of grudges. Unlike boys who can often forgive and forget, or at least forget, girls tend to hold on to disagreements and feel a sense of injustice if the outcome isn't what they desire.

Why Girl Grudges Hurt

Girls are vulnerable to grudges because from birth on, they are oriented toward relationships in a way boys are not. A sense of rejection or hurt by a peer often manifests as anger which gets turned inward or deflected toward others because girls usually do not feel as free as boys to express conflict. When asked, very few girls describe themselves aggressive or see their actions as cruel or wrong. While we know boys use hurtful behaviors with each other, they often tend to "let go" more readily, and may not carry the wounds of rejection or a lifetime grudge.

What You See In a Girl Grudge

There may or may not be obvious signs that two or more girls are involved in a grudge. We have seen the following dynamics:

- Girls may be close friends or distant acquaintances
- An obvious event may start the conflict
- The response of one girl often shapes behavior of other(s), reinforcing negativism
- Ongoing conflict can suck up energy of the group
- Refusal to give up hostility and resentment focuses attention on one girl, which may be her underlying motivation
- Persistent conflict can create a bully-victim-bystander dynamic

Relational Aggression Versus Grudges

Relational aggression (RA), sometimes known as female bullying, can involve many of the same behaviors as grudges. Here is a partial list of behaviors girls identify as RA, or the kind of bullying that never involves a punch or kick, but which can wound far deeper.

Gossip: Deliberately spreading information about another girl with ill intent

Manipulation: Trying to get another girl to do something you want her to do just so you'll be her friend

Intimidation: Threatening to withdraw friendship

Humiliation: Making fun of another girl

Exclusion: Shutting another girl out

Gestures: Eye rolling, laughing, sighing, elbowing, and other behaviors that signal dislike

Take-backs: Saying something mean then pretending you were "joking

Name calling: Attaching a derogatory name to another girl

Teasing: A more subtle form of making fun of someone but pretending it isn't really a put down

Cliques: Girls who group together and shut others out

Campaigns: Rallying others against one or more girls

Shifting loyalties: Pretending to be good friends one day and not the next

Betraying confidences: Sharing secrets and confidences that make another person(s) look bad

Other subtle or not so subtle forms of harassment such as online RA where Instant Messages (IMs), web posts, emails, and other types of technology (text messages) are used to perpetuate ill will between girls.

Relational aggression is more common among girls and seems to increase in the middle school years when peers become all-important. These behaviors become the weapons involved in girl grudges, used by a bully/aggressor to initiate the hurt. Victims are the target of her malice, and then there are usually many bystander girls, who witness the situation and may or may not join in.

Features of a Grudge

We believe grudges involve many relationally aggressive behaviors in that a grudge is an intentional focused hate that is often tied to a perceived emotional deficit or previous hurt within the begrudger. A further difference between relational aggression and an ongoing grudge is like comparing a scratch and a wound. RA is often the external manifestation of conflict, while a grudge is the ongoing internal piece of what's lacking or unresolved inside the begrudger.

Some other differences are that RA can be impulsive and self limiting and focused on a different target each day, while grudges tend to be sustained and deep-rooted. It's also possible to have a "quiet" grudge, where the begrudged has no idea she is the target of hostility and resentment. This situation occurs when the begrudger acts "nice" on the surface and things seem fine, but inside, there are intense negative feelings that will never be resolved.

The Life of a Grudge

Grudges take effort! Much negative emotion is invested in maintaining a grudge when you think about it:

- The root of bitterness buried deep inside at least one of the parties involved in the grudge takes up a lot of internal "space."
- Life can become all about the grudge, requiring a lot of energy each day to keep it going, especially if the feelings are kept hidden.
- The begrudger must continue to convince herself that she is completely justified in her feelings and behavior.
- Most of the time, the grudge doesn't have anything to do with the begrudged and everything to do with the begrudger, who has a self-concept that skews her view of reality. (In other situations, a condition called hostile attribution leads a girl to automatically attach an evil intent to the actions of others.)

So why do girls start and maintain grudges, given all this intensity? Consider Maslow's hierarchy of needs (Maslow, 1954, 1971; Maslow & Lowrey, 1998), which shows just how important safety is: it ranks just above our basic physical requirements for food and shelter. Sure, protection from bodily injury is important, but the girl who feels she has been threatened emotionally—whether that perception is correct—can construct all kinds of emotional barriers to protect herself.

Unfortunately, once started, grudges can become a self reinforcing cycle of negative behaviors and responses that fuel the fire of resentment and hostility.

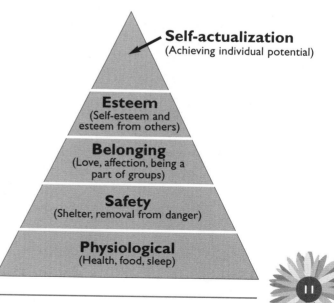

Self-actualization
(Achieving individual potential)

Esteem
(Self-esteem and esteem from others)

Belonging
(Love, affection, being a part of groups)

Safety
(Shelter, removal from danger)

Physiological
(Health, food, sleep)

Understanding Grudges

Activity #1:
Can You Budge That Grudge?

Objectives:
Upon completion of this activity, girls will:
- Gain insight into their beliefs about grudges
- Discuss differences in grudges
- Examine the relevance of grudges to girl relationships

Procedure:
Each of us has our own beliefs about grudges—what they are, who they involve, and how they play out. To explore these ideas further, make copies of the *Defining A Grudge worksheet*. Have girls fold the worksheet in half and complete the top section only. Number one is to be answered from the individual girl's point of view. Number two is based on what other girls have to say (allow a few minutes for girls to interview each other). Number three is based on an official definition such as the one found in a dictionary (have several handy).

After the top section is finished, discuss how much agreement or disagreement there is between answers. Since differences of opinions are often at the heart of a grudge, this is an opportunity to role model positive communication skills. Stress that there are no "right" or "wrong" answers to the questions, and encourage each girl to share what she has written.

Next, flip the paper and complete the bottom section of the worksheet, Grudge Survey. repeating the process of sharing answers and maintaining an "okay to disagree" environment. Although a case could be made for either agreement or disagreement with each statement, boys do hold grudges, physical fighting can be a part of grudges, it's not always apparent when two girls strongly dislike each other, grudges can last for years, and gangs are often held together by a shared grudge.

Defining A Grudge

My Opinion

1. What is a grudge? Write your definition below:

_____

_____

_____

Others Opinion

2. Here are some thoughts of other girls about grudges:

_____

_____

_____

Official Definition

3. Here is the official definition of a grudge:

_____

_____

_____

Grudge Survey

Check whether you agree or disagree with each statement.

☐ Agree ☐ Disagree   Grudges are more of a problem for girls than boys

☐ Agree ☐ Disagree   Girls can get into physical fights because of grudges

☐ Agree ☐ Disagree   It's always obvious when two girls hate each other

☐ Agree ☐ Disagree   Grudges don't go on for longer than a month

☐ Agree ☐ Disagree   One gang of girls can have a grudge against another gang

Understanding Grudges

Activity #2:
A Grudge Quiz

Objectives:
Upon completion of this activity, girls will:
- Gain insight into their own attitudes and beliefs about grudges
- Discuss factual information about grudges
- Identify personal difficulties experienced because of grudges

Procedure:
Read the questions on the worksheet out loud and have girls write a "T" if they believe the statement is True or an "F" is they think it is false. Then ask the girls to briefly write about the reason why they answered as they did in the space underneath each question. Discuss these using the answer key below.

Answer Key
False: Grudges can be the fault of many people, as happens when one clique or one gang of girls has ongoing resentment or conflict with another.
False: Both girls and boys hold grudges, but grudges mean something different to girls.
False: Adults do hold grudges—sometimes all their lives.
True: Sometimes a girl can act nice to your face, but have a grudge against you inside.
False: Sometimes grudges occur because your parents or other adults have the same grudge, and pass it on to you.

Give girls five sheets of blank paper. Ask them to give an example of each of the statements on the worksheet using words, symbols, or art. They should use one sheet of paper for each question.

See if others can decipher the art or writing and guess the answers to the "example" questions. After a dialogue about the uniqueness of grudges to each individual, try to create another set of True and False grudge questions.

A Grudge True or False Test

☐ TRUE ☐ FALSE   Grudges are the fault of one girl, so she is the one who should be held accountable.

☐ TRUE ☐ FALSE   Grudges are more common between girls than boys.

☐ TRUE ☐ FALSE   Grown ups do not get involved in grudges.

☐ TRUE ☐ FALSE   Sometimes, someone can have a grudge against you and you might not even know it.

☐ TRUE ☐ FALSE   Grudges are always the cause of something that happened in the past.

Give an example of:

1. Grudges between two or more groups of people: _____

_____

2. How girls feel about grudges and how boys feel: _____

_____

3. A lifelong grudge: _____

_____

4. A grudge that wasn't obvious: _____

_____

5. A grudge that your parents or someone else "passed along" to you:

_____

_____

Understanding Grudges

Activity #3:
The Grudge That Wouldn't End

Objectives:
Upon completion of this activity, girls will:
- Learn about different types of grudges
- Compare and contrast different types of grudges
- Discuss motivation for grudges

Procedure:
Read each of the following stories about girl grudges, stopping to answer the questions after each one. End with the list of final discussion questions:

Chandra and Mai are best friends throughout elementary school. In sixth grade, Chandra "steals" Frankie, Mai's boyfriend of two months, at a party Mai isn't allowed to attend. (Mai had specifically asked Chandra to look out for Frankie, but things ended up growing intimate when Frankie misunderstood Chandra's behavior.) Mai was furious as soon as she found out what happened and immediately began to IM all her friends, saying Chandra was a "slut" who was boy crazy. Although Chandra apologized and tried to be friends again, Mai refused to forgive her and to this day the girls do not speak.

- Who held the grudge, and why?

- What did the grudge "cost" the girls involved?

- Why do you think the grudge occurred?

Understanding Grudges

Activity #3: (continued)
The Grudge That Wouldn't End

Olivia and Terese have never met, but their older sisters have been arch enemies since freshman year of high school, when they got into a physical fight and Olivia's sister, Brianna, broke Terese's sister Isabelle's nose. Although Olivia and Terese are in the same classes, they both "talk trash" about the other and don't speak face-to-face. Every night, Isabelle tells Terese that she must get "revenge" by fighting Olivia, but Terese is afraid because Olivia is much bigger and stronger than her.

- Who held the grudge, and why?
- What did the grudge "cost" the girls involved?
- Why do you think the grudge occurred?

Andrea comes from a single parent family where money is tight. Most of her clothes are hand-me-downs, and she is part of the free school lunch program. She lives in "The Heights," a part of town known for crime and rundown housing, while her classmate Tiffany lives in a development called nicknamed "Pill Hill" because it is full of doctors. Tiffany's parents have told her since childhood that she must be very careful of her friends, and one time would not allow her to invite Andrea to her birthday party. Now Tiffany and Andrea are in tenth grade, and Tiffany has decided to turn everyone in the school against Andrea. She makes fun of Andrea's clothes and encourages her friends to do the same. At lunch she laughs and tells everyone Andrea can only get certain food because she's on the "free food ticket."

- Who held the grudge, and why?
- What did the grudge "cost" the girls involved?
- Why do you think the grudge occurred?

Understanding Grudges

Activity #3: (continued)
The Grudge That Wouldn't End

Felice is Black, Ann is White, and Carmen is Hispanic. The girls have attended the same school since first grade and all play basketball on the same team, but each of them believes they can never be friends. Felice's mother has told her she can't trust White or Hispanic people, and to stick with her own color. Ann's parents have no friends of color, and frequently comment on how the world has become a worse place since Black and Hispanic people "took over." Carmen's family is new to the country; both of her parents stress that her primary loyalty is to her large extended family. "Black girls are always in trouble and no White girl will be a true friend to you," they tell her. Consequently, Felice, Ann, and Carmen each mistrust each other and rarely speak unless they have to. At times, there has been obvious tension between them in basketball games when each believes the others are "hogging" the ball or playing only for themselves.

- Who held the grudge, and why?

- What did the grudge "cost" the girls involved?

- Why do you think the grudge occurred?

Final Discussion Questions:

- What do these grudges have in common?

- What behaviors kept the grudges going?

- Who was hurt by the grudges?

- What could have been done to overcome each grudge?

Understanding Grudges

Activity #4:
The Care and Keeping of a Grudge

Objectives:
Upon completion of this activity, girls will:
- Recognize behaviors associated with perpetuating a grudge
- Discuss the energy it takes to keep a grudge going
- Describe the negative consequences of maintaining a grudge

Procedure:
Think about a grudge, such as the one described below, or one of your own. Let's go through a typical day in the life of both the begrudger (initiator of the grudge) and the begrudged (target of the grudge). Then complete the worksheet on the following page.

TIME OF DAY	BEGRUDGER (SHARON)	BEGRUDGED (JULIA)
6 A.M.-7 A.M.	Sharon wakes up, instantly angered and upset at the thought of something Julia posted online the night before.	Julia wakes up, instantly upset and feels intimidated by the thought of seeing Sharon at school.
8 A.M.-9 A.M.	Sharon goes to school, looking for someone who will listen to her rant about Julia, and watching for some behavior Julia displays that will reinforce the grudge, which began two years ago when Julia made the cheer-leading squad and she didn't.	Julia thinks about going to the school nurse because she feels sick with dread over seeing Sharon. She knows something is wrong in her relationship with Sharon but isn't sure what she did to prompt it.
10 A.M.-12 P.M.	Sharon can't concentrate in class because she is busy anticipating what will come next with the grudge. In the cafeteria, she points at Julia and attempts to get other girls to join her in laughing and making rude comments.	Julia is preoccupied in class, trying to figure out how she will avoid Sharon. She sets herself up for further resentment by asking another friend why Sharon is upset with her. That "friend" runs to Sharon with this news.
2 P.M.-3 P.M.	Sharon leaves school, already contemplating how she will further her grudge against Julia during the evening hours.	Julia goes home, where she is afraid to turn computer on and see if Sharon has posted anything about her.
4 P.M.-10 P.M.	Sharon calls and IMs any one she might consider a friend, trying to get them involved in her grudge against Julia by telling them negative things Julia has supposedly said or done in the past.	Julia begins to receive hostile phone calls and emails, accusing her of being disloyal or hostile to other girls at her school she doesn't even know very well. Some of the messages are threatening, while others just suggest she should never come back to school.
11 P.M.	Sharon goes to bed but can't sleep because she is still upset about Julia and her inability to get revenge on her. She lies awake, plotting new ways to attack Julia the next day.	Julia goes to bed and cries herself to sleep because she can't understand why all the girls at her school hate her so much.

Grudge Day Worksheet

Now think about a grudge you or someone you know are involved in, and complete the following chart:

Time of Day	Begrudger	Begrudged
6 A.M.-7 A.M.		
8 A.M.-9 A.M.		
10 A.M.-12 P.M.		
2 P.M.-3 P.M.		
4 P.M.-10 P.M.		
11 P.M.		

Understanding Grudges

Activity #5:
Body Symptom Checklist

Objectives:
Upon completion of this activity, girls will:
- Learn about the connection between negative emotions and physical feelings
- Discuss how feelings influence behavior
- Describe consequences of prolonged grudges

Procedure:
There is a big connection between negative emotions and how our bodies feel at any given moment, although we often aren't aware of it. Take a small empty bag and a stack of used paper, or have girls imagine doing such. Begin by wadding up one piece of paper and putting it in the bag. It's pretty easy to fit it in, at first. Continue wadding up pieces of paper and stuffing them in the bag until they won't fit any more without splitting open. People are the same way—they eventually reach a point where they just can't hold one more negative emotion.

Have girls complete the *Feelings Check Up worksheet*. If they checked any of these it could be an example of the connection between what goes on in your brain and your body. If they didn't check any of these, what other things might they notice about the relationship between their health and their feelings? For example, ask: "Are you always tired, sick, or otherwise less than healthy?" and "Do you notice a connection between your thoughts and feelings and how your body functions?"

Next, have girls check words on the bottom of the next page that they have experienced in relation to a grudge. Expect to have a discussion around what each word means, and allow girls to offer definitions. Add any other emotion words they might feel.

Encourage girls to think about each of those feelings and describe how they respond physically to them. For example, sometimes feeling afraid makes a girl's stomach upset, and sometimes anger causes tenseness in your body.

To continue raising awareness, have girls to keep track of how they are feeling emotionally and physically in the next week using copies of the *How I Feel From Day To Day worksheet*. See if they can identify a connection between the two. They can rate themselves once a day or more on a scale of 1-5, with 1 being "feeling as bad as possible" and 5 being "feeling as good as possible."

22

Feelings Check Up

Give yourself a check mark for each statement that applies to you:

❑ When I feel anxious about a test, I have trouble sleeping.

❑ If I have an argument with my mom, I can't think about anything else.

❑ When I'm upset I often get a stomachache or headache.

❑ When I have something to look forward to, I don't feel as tired or uncomfortable as usual.

❑ If I have a bad day at school, I have trouble sleeping.

❑ When something wonderful happens, I feel as if I get extra energy.

A GRUDGE MAKES ME FEEL:

❑ Angry   ❑ Confused   ❑ Vengeful

❑ Resentful   ❑ Enraged   ❑ Depressed

❑ Hostile   ❑ Hurt   ❑ Fearful

❑ Jealous   ❑ Stubborn   ❑ Righteous

❑ Other: _____

How I Feel From Day To Day

Today's Date: _____

Time Completed: _____

Use the rating scale of 1-5 below:
1="I feel as bad as possible"
2="I feel pretty bad"
3="I feel just okay"
4= "I feel good"
5="I feel as good as possible"

Rate how you feel physically: _____

Rate how you feel emotionally: _____

Describe what was going on right before you completed this page:

_____

_____

_____

_____

_____

_____

Section Two
RELATE

Take a Look at Yourself

While some grudges involve an obvious transgressor (the begrudger), and their victims (the begrudged), all too often, the dynamic of grudges isn't so straightforward and roles get confused. A complex pattern evolves that ends up being more interactive than unidirectional.

Every person on the face of the earth has the potential to be involved in some kind of grudge--stories of this kind of unyielding conflict dating back to the origin of time. For a modern day version, one only has to pick up a newspaper and read a report of clashes between cultures, gangs, or individuals.

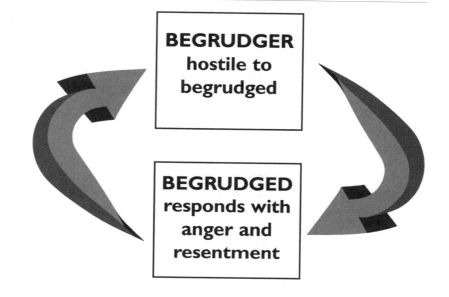

BEGRUDGER hostile to begrudged

BEGRUDGED responds with anger and resentment

Consider these girl grudges and see whether they sound familiar:

#1: Loyalty Grudge: She won't be friends with someone her best friend doesn't like. She doesn't like you because her friends don't like you.

#2: Queen Bee Grudge: It's all about her: you hurt her so she campaigns against you.

#3: Inadvertent Grudge: You did something wrong but you don't know what it is and she stops speaking to you.

#4: Learned Grudge: My older sister or mom doesn't like x, y, z so I won't either.

#5: The Unexplainable Grudge: She has to be angry at someone, so you're the one.

#6: The Historical Grudge: You did something to her and she can't let go of it.

#7: The Guy Grudge: She's dating your ex or a boy you secretly like.

These are just a few of the conflicts which can spark the fire of an ongoing grudge in women of any age.

The Big Picture

Just as the motivations for grudges differ, the parties involved can too. They can exist on a micro or macro level, and can be caused by direct or indirect experiences. Consider these examples:

■ **One-on-One:**
In kindergarten, one girl steals another girl's lunch box. From that point on, a deep divide exists between these girls, even though the thief returns the stolen item with a verbal apology. At high school graduation, the same girls refuse to even congratulate each other because of an incident that occurred over a decade ago.

■ **Group-to-Group:**
These kinds of grudges can occur on many levels, with groups of girls squaring off against each other. The "Goths vs. Preps" or "Cheerleaders vs. Geeks" rivalries are ones we frequently hear about, but the possibilities are endless. Most of the girls in the sparring groups may not even feel all that strongly about maintaining the hostility, but the group identity is so intertwined with the grudge it's hard to turn things around.

■ **Institution vs. Institution:**
Think of schools that have an ongoing grudge with one or two other schools close by. The schools may be separated by different socioeconomic or demographic status, or nearly identical in profile, but the hostility is real. There can be good natured tests of sports or academic ability between school rivals, but when the emotions ignite into more, no one is having fun.

■ **Community vs. Community:**
Even neighborhoods and communities can have labels attached that divide them. Assuming that all girls who live in a particular area are rich or poor, smart or dumb, or any other quality shuts down relationships and perpetuates grudges.

Grudges involving any number of people can arise out of prejudice, which is an opinion based on stereotyped perceptions of that person or group. Sometimes, something as simple as an individual or group attitude can be a manifestation of a grudge.

Outcomes of Grudges

Unfortunately, grudges can result in outcomes which impact negatively on both our mental and physical health. The STUCK acronym can explain some of the outcomes of grudges:

Stubborn

Traumatic

Unresolved

Conflict

Knotted

■ **Stubborn:**
Girls who fall prey to a grudge lifestyle can carry this trait into adulthood. It can make them difficult to live with, because the expression "My way or no way" applies without exception, and can destroy friendships as well as relationships with family members, coworkers, etc.

■ **Traumatic:**
Regardless of whether you begin the grudge or are the target of it, the feelings of hurt can persist for a lifetime—especially if you don't understand why the grudge occurs. Emotional wounds are often translated into physical problems such as depression, substance abuse, and eating disorders.

■ **Unresolved:**
It's very difficult to leave behind "unfinished business." Many women long for a second chance to go back and undo the damage of a childhood grudge, but no longer have that opportunity. It will make you a different person to carry the burden of a grudge that never got resolved.

■ **Conflict:**
Like a tiny pebble in your shoe, ongoing conflict is a daily irritant. Over time, you may think you won't notice it, but the constant irritation and discomfort can manifest in your every day behavior.

■ **Knotted:**
Due to the convoluted nature of grudges, one girl's feelings are often intertwined with another. It becomes difficult if not impossible to figure out who or what started the grudge. This lack of clarity about cause and effect can even lead to various somatic complaints that manifest as headaches, fatigue, and stomach aches. Another "K" that applies is the word "Killer." Sad but true, ongoing grudges can lead to actual physical trauma and even violence. Girls are different than boys in that they tend to build up to an act of physical aggression with an ongoing grudge that can't or won't be resolved, rather than acting on impulse. Once that fatal blow is struck, there's no turning back.

27

As described in the STUCK model, there are many unfortunate outcomes that can result from grudges, some on a short term basis and others more pervasive. Some situations we have seen that involved girls who were STUCK include:

■ "The Lost Opportunity:"

Holly met Serena at one of our programs for girls. Instantly, Holly looked at Serena, and, based on her appearance, automatically ruled out the possibility of a friendship between them. Holly's judgment of Serena was in reality also a judgment of herself. For example, when a girl judges someone's looks and chooses to dislike her, it might be due to insecurity about her own looks. This results in a missed opportunity for a relationship between both girls.

■ "Missed Chances to Resolve Conflict:"

We once worked with a young woman, Margaret, who declared quite adamantly during a discussion about relational aggression at her school: "Things will never change. Girls at my school will always be mean." It was clear Margaret's opinions were fixed and even if the opportunity arose, we wondered if she would open herself to the possibility of change.

■ "Rigid Thinking/Lack of Flexibility:"

Susan was a girl who could never admit that she was wrong about anything, or that her behaviors were hurtful and aggressive. Although others saw Susan as a bully, in her mind, she believed her actions were completely justified—her stock phrase was: "She deserved it." Although Susan described being the target of bullying from others in the past, she refused to believe her current inter- action style was in any way similar to that of her tormentors.

■ "Poor Communication Skills:"

Misunderstandings and assumptions can fuel a grudge. For example, one year at Camp Ophelia, Della, an adolescent camper, was sure another camper, Tricia, was deliberately trying to antagonize her. Della gave her mentor several examples of Tricia's behavior; she stared at Della, asked her stupid questions, and followed her around. As camp continued, Della grew more and more hostile toward Tricia until it was revealed that Tricia was Della's "secret sister," assigned to learn as much about her as she could without being too obvious. In this situation, Della had the grace to admit to a breakdown in communication skills: she had misread Tricia's behavior. Not all girls are so easily convinced to pause and reflect on a situation, or to talk things out with others.

■ "Misrepresentation of Self:"

Alicia is a teenaged girl who is stuck in the grudge way of life, constantly projecting an impression that may not be true. Everyone who meets Alicia thinks she is tough and self-confident, ready to defend herself verbally and physically against others. No one knows that inside, Alicia is really terrified someone will attack her.

■ "Out to Get Me:"

Laurie, another teen, often misinterprets the actions and words of others. She never fails to see the world in a threatening way and expects the worse to happen. This leads to a mindset where other girls are always viewed as potential enemies rather than friends, and inclines her to become stuck in the role of victim/begrudged.

■ **"Negative, Negative, Negative:"**

Brittany has an opinion about everything, and it's always negative. She sees only bad intentions in other girls, and portrays this with both her words and body language: rolling her eyes, turning her head the other way, or sighing loudly when her peers are speaking. She will always see the glass as half empty rather than half full, making her prone to a grudging interaction style with others, and vice versa.

■ **"Skewed World View:"**

Chronic grudges can have girls leapfrogging from one grudge to another, as happened with Lacey. In elementary school, Lacey had problems with girls who she thought were ugly. By middle school, this translated into girls whom she thought were pretty, as well as the unattractive. In high school, she had an instant dislike for girls who were thin, unattractive, or pretty. In each case, Lacey used the grudge in a misguided attempt to alleviate her own sense of insecurity. Her dislike of others gave her a false sense of personal superiority.

It Happened to Us

None of us are immune from the fallout of grudges. In working with others to resolve the ongoing hurt, it's important to recognize that grudges have impacted your own life. As girls, we both can remember experiences with grudges.

CHERYL...

The most memorable grudge I remember occurred in nursing school. Before that, I had experienced grudges because I was a cheerleader in high school, a jock, a recluse, and a number of other titles that others attached to me. I also held grudges—I can remember how hard it was to forgive the girl who "stole" my date to the Sadie Hawkins dance—I still know her name and exactly what she looked like!

J. was different. She was a girl I was forced into fairly close contact with during college because we had many classes together and our rooms were right around the hall from each other. Mistakenly, I thought J. liked me—we often worked together on assignments and she was always pleasant to my face, although she didn't go out of her way to be friendly. Imagine my shock when another mutual friend told me J. literally hated my guts! The "friend" went on to describe all the things J. had said about me. During the many months when I thought J. and I were working well together, she had secretly been rolling her eyes and belittling me to every girl in our dorm. I confronted J. about what I had learned, and although she denied it, I had heard her talking about other girls in mean and spiteful ways. To this day, I don't believe J. was deliberately being hurtful, but I know for the rest of the time I was forced to work with her, I never let my guard down around her again.

SHILESTE...

I was in 7th grade, already feeling like I didn't quite fit in, but my best friend was the most popular girl in school, so everyone thought that I was as strong and confident as she was. A particular girl, I'll call "Lisa" hated me. She used to call me all kinds of names, make threats to physically attack me, roll her eyes, and suck her teeth when she saw me coming down the hall. I had never even done anything to this girl and didn't really even know her. The name calling and the other negative behaviors persisted all the way through the end of my eighth grade year, when finally I confronted her and asked her what her problem was with me. She really couldn't answer, but just responded with; "You think you're so cute."

Assessing the Personal Impact of Grudges

Activity #6:
Making It Right

Objectives:
Upon completion of this activity, girls will:
- Use writing to express emotions about a grudge
- Explore the impact of a grudge on all parties involved
- Describe the behaviors involved in a grudge

Procedure:
Ask girls to think about a "famous" grudge. (If they get stuck, almost any article from a popular tabloid that describes ongoing feuds between female starlets will illustrate nicely.) They could also think about characters in a book or groups of people. Have them write a few sentences that describe:
- What you know about the grudge?
- Do you feel one person is more "right" or "wrong" than the other?
- If you were asked to resolve the grudge, what would you do?
- How could you make everyone involved in the grudge change their hurtful behavior?
- Is there anything positive about the grudge?

Now have them write about a real life situation where someone experienced either a short or long term grudge. Make sure real names or identifying details aren't used, and don't have them sign the story (if used in a group). Once completed, fold the papers in quarters and give to the leader. Shuffle the papers and exchange the stories. Read them out loud and then discuss:
- Who did the grudge effect?
- How did the grudge impact on everyone involved?
- Who had the power to resolve the grudge?
- Now create a new ending to the story that would "make it right."

Assessing the Personal Impact of Grudges

Activity #7:
Fairy Tale

Objectives:

Upon completion of this activity, girls will:
- Reevaluate stories from their youth which may shape attitudes about grudges
- Compare "fairy tale" grudges with real life grudges
- Change the ending of a traditional fairy tale

Procedure:

Many of the stories we grow up with tell the same story: women act badly and men are the heroes. Think of Cinderella, Snow White, and Sleeping Beauty, to name a few. In each, one or more women have negative feelings toward the central figure of the story. Cinderella's stepsisters and stepmother resent her because she was her father's only child, forced into their family by marriage. Snow White's stepmother also resented her for her beauty, which led to a near fatal grudge. Sleeping Beauty also was the victim of an evil minded female. (If you have copies of these stories, read them out loud.) Have girls share other "fairy tales" they may know of where grudges predominate.

The aggressors in each of these fairy tales held onto sustained negative feelings for reasons that were often not based in reality. While the men were heroes and rescuers, the women were the cause of serious problems that could have even led to the death of another person. Research shows that men are much more likely to harm each other physically, but that's not the way these fairy tales go.

Select one of the three stories mentioned and discuss how superficial behaviors reinforced the underlying grudge and the motivations of each character. Next, create a version of the fairy tale where the grudge is resolved without hurtful behaviors on the part of the women involved. What things have to change?

Finally, have them create yet another version of the fairy tale in which the grudge never gets a chance to happen. How were they able to make that happen?

Challenge them to write a modern day fairy tale on the worksheet that has a magical but positive story about women and their relationships with each other.

Assessing the Personal Impact of Grudges

Activity #8:
Gauge Your Grudge Quiz

Objectives:
Upon completion of this activity, girls will:
- Understand their "grudge potential"
- Identify areas where grudges have had a negative influence on their lives
- Discuss what was at the heart of the grudge

Procedure:
First, have girls take the Grudge-Ability Quiz below to explore how grudges have impacted on them. Once finished, use the Key to discuss answers. The text in italics that follows each item is a guide to get girls talking about how grudges have negatively influenced their lives, and what might underlie grudges.

Key

I can remember fights I had with other girls that took place many years ago. (Disagree).
Negative events that get "cemented" in our minds have the ability to continue hurting us. If you agreed with this question, ask yourself what it would take to "let go" of the hurtful memories you have, and whether you are holding on to other events from the immediate and distant past that are making your life less enjoyable.

It's easy for me to make up with my friends after we have an argument. (Agree).
If you are able to use the important life skill of conflict resolution and forgiveness by figuring out ways to reconcile differences, you are a girl who has an advantage that will help you now in your friendships and later in your career.

I don't hold grudges—it's not in my nature. (Agree)
Having a temperament that allows you to shrug off resentment and ongoing hostility against others helps spare a lot of negative emotions in your life. If you aren't naturally easygoing and forgiving, it is a skill you can learn.

Once someone offends me, that's it. They'll never be my friend again. (Disagree)
We all offend others. If you agreed with this item, take some time to think about whether you have ever done something to hurt or offend another. Be honest—we all have. Were you ever given a second chance at a friendship? If you were, why not extend the same opportunity to others? If you weren't given a second chance, you know how hard it is to live with a grudge.

I found out a friend had a grudge against me and it really hurt my feelings.
I didn't even know she hated me. (Either).
Being genuine is an important part of any relationship—even if it doesn't involve feelings of friendship. Girls who are not what they seem to be can make you uncomfortable. If you've had this happen to you, take some time to write about who has acted with integrity in the hurtful situation: you, the person who has a grudge against you but hid it, or, if there was a third person who felt it necessary to tell you about the deception, that person. If you haven't had this happen to you, list behaviors that help girls know others are really their friends.

Activity #8:
Gauge Your Grudge Quiz (continued)

Grudges are exciting. I would never start one myself, but I do watch when they happen. (Disagree)
A grudge often continues because of all the "bystanders" or watchers who passively participate in the hostility. Listening to negative comments or even not objecting or walking away can give the person who starts the grudge the impression you approve of her behavior.

If a girl really hurts me, she does not deserve my forgiveness. (Disagree).
While it may seem only right that a girl who offended you be paid back in some way for hurting you, you'll quickly exhaust yourself if you spend your life withholding your forgiveness from every person who hurts your feelings. You don't have to "kiss and make up" or even believe the other person's actions were right in any way to forgive her. Letting go of your sense of anger, betrayal, and hurt over her behavior will not only free you to move on with your life, it will improve your health.

Girls who provoke me deserve what they get. (Disagree).
Stop for a moment and define what the word "provoke" means to you. What kinds of thing do and don't provoke you? The list will be different for every girl on this earth. Now make a list of the kinds of things you do that might provoke others, and think about what you might "deserve" to have happen to you if that happens. It's also possible that other girls may not realize they are "provoking" you—they may mistakenly believe you like their attentions, even if they're not kind ones. Consider the options you have to check out a girl's intentions the next time you are on the receiving end of seemingly hostile behavior.

I'm not like other girls who hold grudges. (Neutral).
Describe the typical girl who holds a grudge. Is she popular or not, smart or not, the same age, height, and weight as you? In reality, there is no "typical" girl who holds a grudge—anyone is capable of it. Even if you aren't currently involved in a grudge situation, you and all the girls you know have the potential to be. You might believe you are somehow more justified in holding a grudge than other girls, or unique or different in other ways, but it's simply not true since deep inside, every girl with a grudge harbors a sense of ongoing negative emotion they refuse to give up.

It's okay to hold a grudge as long as no one knows about it. (Disagree).
Grudges are actually bad for your health! Even if you think it's okay to hold a grudge as long as you're not overtly hostile towards others, you are still hurting yourself with the negative emotions buried deep inside. Racism often has its roots in the belief that it's okay to resent black, white, or any other kind of person, as long as you don't act on your beliefs. Studies have shown that refusing to let go of negative grudging emotions is connected with a number of health conditions such as high blood pressure and depression. Also consider that the feelings you believe are "secret" often slip out in stereotyping statements, such as: "White people are sneaky," or "Black people are more aggressive." Right now, the only universal statements that can be made about anyone is that they're either male or female, were born, and will die someday!

If time permits, create your own "grudge quiz' and test it out on other girls.

Your Grudge-Ability

For each item, indicate if you Agree or Disagree.

☐ Agree ☐ Disagree I can remember fights I had with girls years ago

☐ Agree ☐ Disagree It's easy for me to make up with my friends after we have an argument

☐ Agree ☐ Disagree I don't hold grudges—it's not in my nature

☐ Agree ☐ Disagree Once someone offends me, that's it. They'll never be my friend again.

☐ Agree ☐ Disagree I found out a friend had a grudge against me and it really hurt my feelings. I didn't even know she hated me.

☐ Agree ☐ Disagree Grudges are exciting. I would never start one myself, but I do watch when they happen to others.

☐ Agree ☐ Disagree If a girl really hurts me, she does not deserve my forgiveness.

☐ Agree ☐ Disagree Girls who provoke me deserve what they get.

☐ Agree ☐ Disagree I'm not like other girls who hold grudges.

☐ Agree ☐ Disagree It's okay to hold a grudge as long as no one knows about it.

34

Understanding Grudges

Activity #9:
The Heart of the Matter

Objectives:
Upon completion of this activity, girls will:
- List five common motivations behind grudges
- Assess their personal motivations around grudges
- Discuss other factors that influence grudges

Procedure:
Below are five common reasons why grudges often occur:
1. One girl is jealous or resentful of another
2. One girl has been hurt by another
3. Parents or influential others "teach" a girl that grudges are appropriate
4. A misperception or false belief initiates or perpetuates a grudge
5. One girl assumes another girl has done something deliberately to offend her

Are there any other reasons not listed?

Make copies of the *Heart of The Matter* worksheet and discuss what each word means. Give an example of how each can cause a grudge, and add any others that aren't listed. Discuss your results.

The Heart Of The Matter

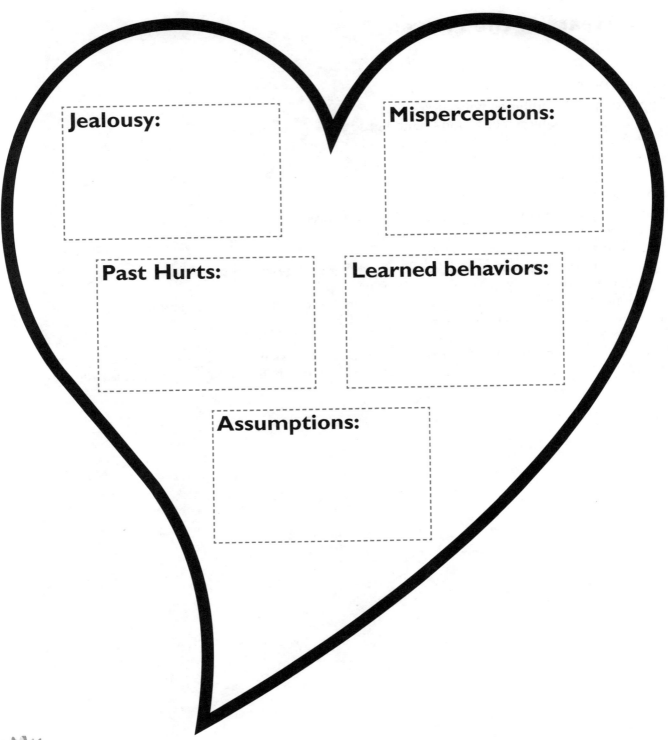

Jealousy:

Misperceptions:

Past Hurts:

Learned behaviors:

Assumptions:

Understanding Grudges

Activity #10:
Tug of War

Objectives:
Upon completion of this activity, girls will:
- Explore the roles of begrudged and begrudger
- Develop empathy for both the begrudger and begrudged
- Identify how the power and strength of others impacts on grudges

Procedure:
You will need an eight foot long piece of sturdy rope and tape for this activity. This is a group activity which requires at least six girls, plenty of space, and a soft floor.

Explain the dynamics of a grudge, including the difference between a begrudger and a begrudged. Select five girls to be on one team. They are the "begrudgers." Appoint one girl to be the "main" begrudger. Have the team make up a story as to why they are holding a grudge.

Put a piece of tape on the floor, and appoint one other girl to be the begrudged. Have her stand alone on the opposite side of the "team," and tell them you are going to play a gentle game of tug-of-war. At the "go" signal, see if the team can pull the single girl across the line of tape. Of course, the five girls will be stronger and "win" easily, but is there any way the one begrudged girl might be able to win? (Hint—four of the girls on the team refuse to pull, leaving the main begrudger on her own.)

Now allow the begrudged girl to "recruit" three girls from the team to join her. She must convince them to join her, playing out the grudge scenario. For example, she might tell them that the begrudger is really talking about them behind their backs, or doesn't really like them.

Now, with a four to two ratio, repeat the tug-of-war activity. Again discuss the predictions of who will win.

Scramble the girls so they are with different teams than before and try again—mix up girls so some of the original begrudgers are with those who joined the begrudged side. Ask how it feels to be teammates with different girls.

Activity #10:
Tug of War *(continued)*

For the last part of this game, select one "begrudger" and one "begrudged." Have them stand separately, and take turns trying to have them convince the freestanding girls to join them, still staying with the grudge scenario. They might say things like:

- "You owe me"
- "You've been my best friend since kindergarten"

and so on. It's important to stay in the characters of the grudge and not lapse into their usual personas.

Allow girls to choose which "grudge" side they want to be on, giving the option of walking away and not making a choice. When and if they do make a choice, ask:

- "What made you join the side you did?"
- "How hard was it to make a decision about which side to join?"
- "Did fear play a role in decision making?"

Answers might be something like:

- "I went with my friends."
- "I picked the side likely to win."
- "I was scared girls wouldn't like me if I went with a particular side."

Discuss how this activity relates to grudges, which can be a real life, invisible tug of war for all involved.

Understanding Grudges

Activity #11:
Meeting in the Middle

Objectives:

Upon completion of this activity, girls will:
- Empathize with both the begrudger and begrudged roles
- Identify behaviors that maintain or end a grudge
- Apply new perspectives to her own situation

Procedure:

Take a large piece of blank paper and have the girl draw a picture of herself on the far left side of the paper, pretending she is at the beginning of a journey. Her drawing can be as simple as a stick figure or more elaborate. Then she should draw a picture of the girl who is involved in a grudge with her on the far right.

Have her write single words that she feels describe how she is feeling, then have her do the same for the other figure on the right, describing her co-grudger or begrudger with single words (or if roles are reversed, adjust accordingly).

Look at whether any of the words describe a similar characteristic. Now, have her write in the middle of the paper words that describe both her and the co-grudger, for example, we are both girls, we are both students at this school, etc. These can be very basic.

Next, ask her to draw a bridge between the two figures, and explore:
- Who is likely to step onto the bridge first?
- What would it take to get each girl to step onto the bridge?
- If neither girl steps onto the bridge, what is likely to happen in the future?

If she wants, she can draw a series of steps leading up to the bridge, and discuss what are the smaller steps that might lead to the bridge, for both her and the other girl. Question what it would take from both sides to keep girls going up those steps and toward the bridge, and what they might say when each reaches the middle.

Understanding Grudges

Activity #12:
Choose Your Own Adventure

Objectives:
Upon completion of this activity, girls will:
- Help empower girls to "write their own story" about the grudge
- Use storytelling as an opportunity to discuss how the grudge has impacted on all girls involved
- Examine personal abilities which can be used to establish positive or neutral connections with others.

Procedure:
Give the girl about ten minutes to write out the story of the grudge she is involved in. Encourage her to be as detailed as possible, and to address the following questions in her writing:
- Who is involved in the grudge?
- Has the impact of this grudge spread beyond the girls most immediately involved?
- Why do you think this grudge has occurred?

For girls who find writing challenging, you can use a tape recorder or computer, or you may choose to be the "scribe" who records her thoughts.

Once the story is completed, discuss the questions above, and then ask her to write about what the situation will look like in a month if nothing changes (meaning neither girl budges and the grudge continues).

After this is done, ask her to write an alternative ending where one of the girls does budge away from the grudge. If that happened, in one month, what would the situation look like? What would it take to make that change happen, and who is likely to be able to do it?

End with a discussion of personal attributes such as compassion, integrity, strength, sense of humor, etc. which can be used to help "rewrite" the story of the grudge, if only for one of the girls involved. Discuss how these attributes might be of use in future situations.

Understanding Grudges

Activity #13:
TV or Not TV

Objectives:

Upon completion of this activity, girls will:
- Examine media messages about women's relationships and how they impact on girls and women
- Explore motivations for female grudges
- Discuss alternative images which portray women positively

Procedure:

Assign girls to watch TV for an evening and give examples of shows where girls are encouraged to develop grudge-like attitudes toward each other. For example, *America's Top Model, My Super Sweet Sixteen,* or *The Bachelor* all pit one woman against each other,
OR

Watch clips from a movie such as *The Parent Trap* or *Bring It On (Parts One and Two)* where ongoing negative behaviors make for excitement and drama,
OR

Gather popular magazines and look at pictures of women, especially in advertisements. When women are featured together, what do their expressions and body language portray about their relationships?
OR

Read passages from books which feature girls who are mean to each other as the prominent dynamic, for example, *The Clique* or *Gossip Girls* series.

Consider the following questions, which have no right or wrong answers. You can either discuss or write about their thoughts, and then share:
- How do you feel when you see these examples?
- Why do you think women are portrayed as enemies in the media?

Ask girls to think of a woman who they consider a role model for others.
- What kind of relationships might she have?
- What would make her a role model?

List three things girls can do to reverse the image of "mean girls" who are hurtful toward each other and prone to grudges. These might include:
- Writing a letter to the editor or producer
- Boycotting television shows or music
- Raising awareness among other girls

Understanding Grudges

Activity #14:
Picture This

Objectives:
Upon completion of this activity, girls will:
- Use images to explore the basis of grudges
- Discuss the life of a grudge
- Express emotions around the grudge

Procedure:
Obtain a stack of assorted women's magazines and have girls go through them and find pictures of as many things as possible which can cause grudges, for example:
- Boys
- Possessions
- Parents
- Others

Use the cut out pictures to create a "grudge collage" that captures the reasons why many grudges occur. Discuss how each image can begin a grudge, and how once started, this kind of a grudge can continue. For example:
- Having an ex-boyfriend date another girl can start a grudge; watching her treat him badly and still having him like her can keep it going.
- Envying someone's wardrobe can begin hostility; seeing a daily change of outfits that cause further jealousy perpetuates it.

Take a pen, pencil, or marker and write words or sentences next to each of the images that captures emotions around the grudge. Acknowledge the reality of these emotions, and discuss how they impact on daily life.

Understanding Grudges

Activity #15:
Map It Out

Objectives:
Upon completion of this activity, girls will:
- Identify how grudges impact all girls involved, even indirectly
- Examine relationships between girls involved in a grudge
- Discuss how girls not directly involved in a grudge can be a resource to help or hurt

Procedure:

In addition to the girl or girls directly involved in a grudge, there are many others around them who are also effected by the negative behaviors, including family members. Too often, we focus on those most immediately involved in the conflict, without considering how others in the social environment can perpetuate or help resolve a grudge. Use the template to create a cluster diagram like this example, which maps out all those involved in a grudge:

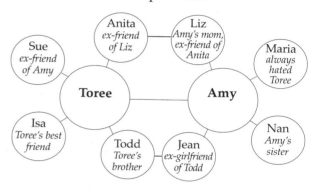

We don't know the "backstory" in the sample cluster map. Did Todd break up with Jen because she was friends with Amy? Did the mothers of both girls sever their relationship because of the grudge between their daughters?

The example is relatively simple, but it could easily be made more detailed by extending the circles to include friends of friends, other family members, etc. The more circles drawn, the better the understanding of the far reaching impact of grudges will be.

On a blank sheet of paper, have the girls create their own grudge relationship map, adding as many circles and lines as needed. Use dotted or slashed lines to indicate where a relationship that has been broken. (Note that the lines between the begrudged and begrudger are still solid because they are still in a relationship, even thought it's a negative one.)

Once the map is created, look at how each person's helpful or hurtful behaviors are related to the grudge in the past, present, and future.

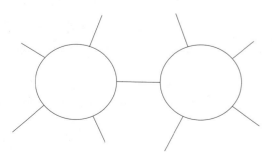

Grudge Relationship Map
Begin with the two girls most immediately involved in the grudge, and add on circles as needed to describe all the people involved in your grudge situation. Add or alter as many lines and circles as needed, or start on a bigger sheet of blank paper and create your own circles.

Interventions to Integrate Change

What to Do

In the emotion of a moment or the midst of a crisis, it is all too easy to act on impulse and do something—anything—that seems like it might help. This section discusses both a clinical and scholarly perspective on interventions so you can benefit from the input of experts when identifying strategies or developing programs for use with girls.

As a professional or a parent, it's important not to become overwhelmed by the need to "solve" a grudge for someone else, perhaps because you have your own painful issues and history with grudges. Before your work with girls, it's helpful to go through the activities yourself, and explore how grudges have impacted on your own life.

One big beginning mistake we hear about from girls is an adult's assumption that a daughter, student, or client's grudge situation is the same as theirs. Too often, as counselors and helpers we try to rationalize or explain away the grudge and its associated hurts and assume the time of resolution has come, but in reality, none of us can force a girl to change when she's not ready. It's also always true that no girl's situation will ever be exactly like ours, or each others.

To understand the basis of integrating the "action oriented" phase of the ERI model, the following information, gathered from clinical and scholarly experts on forgiveness, will provide some scholarly insights on the grudge dynamic. Much of it is culled from the forgiveness literature.

Dr. Jessica Jameson (2007) offers a theory of global conflict that involves three phases of escalation and de-escalation. She calls "intractable conflict" a conflict that persists despite attempts at resolution. Many of her insights are applicable to girl grudges. Her four characteristics of intractable conflict involve: 1) a breakdown in communication between parties, 2) rigid, fixed positions about the conflict and 3) hurtful behaviors between the parties involved, and 4) eventually, a conflict can become a way of life and even comfortable.

According to Jameson (2007) there are also four stages of escalation to a conflict, and three corresponding stages of de-escalation. The genesis of a grudge occurs in this way:

■ **Threat:**
Initially, a person's identity is threatened in some way. How a girl defines herself in relation to her world, and her internal feelings and values may feel threatened. Sometimes, it only takes another girl who is different in some way to prompt a threat.

■ **Distortion:**
A consequence of the feelings in stage one can be defensiveness and protection of the self. Either the information underlying the threat can be rationalized ("She thinks I'm a snob," or "She never liked me") or the judgement of the other party is undermined. ("Who cares what she thinks, anyway?")

■ **Rigidification:**
By this point, a "Me" vs. "Thee" stance is entrenched and unyielding, with other girls see choosing one side or the other as mutually exclusive. The concept "in" and "out" groups arises, as one individual or clique is perceived as somehow superior or better than another.

■ **Collusion:**
At this point, the conflict has been so internalized it is part of the identity of one or both parties involved. The "care and keeping" of a grudge can become the focus of everyday existence, and the girl(s) need to persevere in their belief system in order to maintain their identity. Therefore, I am "Mary in opposition to Susan," rather than "I am Mary."

The good news is grudges can change on various levels. Jameson (2007) suggests these steps:
1. External cues can be enforced that more or less stop the escalation of violent feelings. One girl is made to reconcile with another, or cliques are somehow forced to disband and assimilate with others. While this may be a short term solution, it can be a beginning.
2. Effective dialogue can be implemented between the grudge groups. This involves thinking outside the box and coming up with alternative strategies to get girls who are "at war" with each other interacting in a neutral setting and in more positive ways.
3. A fundamental change in inner identity can be initiated. This helps a girl to release the grudge and reframe perspectives of others. The "that was then, this is now" approach can be valuable. While it sounds easy, for girls in the midst of identity formation, surrendering a deeply held belief that "I am" only in relation to my conflict with "her" can be a bigger process than suggested.

Burgess & Burgess (2003) distinguish between "tractable" and "intractable" conflicts, deeming the latter as those which seem to be irresolvable. Even then, intractable conflict is not a "yes-no" concept but rather a continuum of feelings with easier to resolve conflicts on one end and more challenging ones on the other. The majority fall in between.

These authors describe intractable conflicts as taking on a life of their own, and becoming a self reinforcing cycle where continued aggression reinforces the conflict, sometimes to the point of no return. However, these experts, who direct the Conflict Research Consortium at the University of Colorado, believe all conflict can be changed, if not resolved, given sufficient motivation. In turn, motivation is often participated by perceptions: if both the offender and victim believe the grudge can't be resolved, their attempts to work it out will be less enthusiastic and sincere. Without denying that a grudge exists and injustice may have been done, the Burgess team encourages the idea of a "way out" that enables both parties to look at alternatives.

Nathaniel Wade and Everett Worthington, two authorities and experienced researchers on forgiveness, offer some insights on the process of ending grudges (2003). They point out that most people are uncomfortable having a grudge in their lives, but acknowledge that not everyone is willing to do the hard work of resolution. Religiosity and empathy can be influential, as can the offender's reaction and the nature of the offense.

Logically, a more egregious offense is likely to be harder to forgive. This team makes an interesting distinction between granting forgiveness and the act of being totally cleansed of unforgiveness. Unforgiveness tends to be a delayed reaction that can actually taper off without overt forgiveness.

The degree of forgiveness that persists is often related to the degree of unforgiveness both parties involved in a grudge feel. If there is a sense that the transgressor regrets her actions and feels remorse, the victim is more likely to feel empathic and motivated to forgive. The four steps of forgiveness Wade & Worthington (2003) suggest are to: 1.) Accept the hurt, 2). Reframe the circumstances surrounding the hurt, 3) Manage stress, and 4) Control anger.

Impact on Health

Holding a grudge is not only bad for relationships, it's bad for your health. Van Oyen Witvliet and her colleagues at Hope College in Michigan illustrate how harboring grudges can have a negative impact on how you feel physically as well as mentally (2001). They call the innate process of rehearsing and reliving the hurt "eroding responses" that effect both physical and mental well-being. The key damaging process is the tendency of the victim to keep repeating and reliving the memories of painful experiences.

To address this dynamic, these psychologists suggest that it is important to develop empathy for the perpetrator, and to view her as human and vulnerable, with context circumstances that may explain her actions. They stress that forgiveness doesn't indicate a belief that the person's offending behavior was right, but their studies of the ability to forgive showed that students who harbored grudges were significantly more negative, angry, sad, and less in control--all emotions that have been connected with adverse health consequences such as cardiac problems, immune system impairment, and chronic stress issues.

Worthington and his colleagues (2002) suggest that unforgiveness is related to substance abuse behaviors. The responses a victim experiences may include: "resentment, bitterness, hostility, hatred, anger, and fear," (p. 257). The biological arousal these emotions create, they believe, can trigger the cascade of behaviors that lead to various types of addictions, including eating disorders. This team suggests that forgiveness is most likely to be achieved when the victim can change how they think about their transgressor, perhaps by asking what her mother likes about her. The point of forgiveness is not static but dynamic, with surrendering a bit more forgiveness each day a more realistic goal than sudden total absolution.

Karremans, Van Lange, & Holland (2005) questioned whether the ability to forgive might have an impact that extends beyond the victim and transgressor. They believe the level of forgiveness extended to a person who has directly hurt you might influence the feelings you have for others who aren't offenders. Indeed, in their series of studies on the topic, they found that forgiveness did shape the behavior of the forgiver beyond the immediate grudge situation. A longer time for consideration enhanced forgiveness and as hypothesized, being forgiving predisposed those studied toward an enhanced sense of relatedness to others in general. Therefore, forgiveness can be framed as an important life skill.

How to Forgive and Resolve Grudges

Valorie Burton (2005), a life coach, speaker, and author, discusses what happens when a grudge consumes a person's life. She says holding on to grudges and anger: "..drains your energy, increases your stress level, and diminishes the quality of your everyday life." Believing that "hurting people hurt people," she suggests that recognizing everyone makes mistakes can be healing. Prayer can also help, even if there's not strong motivation to forgive and end the grudge. Other advice she offers includes not allowing any mental space for grudges, and trying to become a detective and to understand why the grudge occurred and continues. She admits that sometimes questions such as: "Do I really need this relationship in my life?" and "Is it time to change the circumstances of my life?" must be honestly examined and answered.

Melissa Tennen (2006) writes on the subject of grudges for the online column Health AtoZ. According to her, grudges that are not released can lead to feelings of resentment and hostility that can continue for months and even years. Other experts support this notion. The negative emotions generated by a grudge can have very real adverse effects on both physical and mental health, too. The process of ending a grudge, Tennen says, is more than just letting go of anger—it involves "owning" an understanding of what took place and deliberately choosing to go back into or walk away from a relationship. She suggests it's helpful to:

- Write out your thoughts to promote clarity and insight
- Try to understand what is motivating all persons involved
- Don't force the issue: wait until the time is right for you to forgive
- Avoid revenge or extracting an apology or justice as your goal
- Talk about your feelings with others

In an analysis of interventions that fostered forgiveness, Wade & Worthington (2005) suggest that many therapy clients are there because of past hurts or victimization. They stress that forgiveness is often misunderstood as acceptance or overlooking of the transgression. After reviewing scholarly writings about forgiveness, they identify these elements as most common interventions:

- Exploring what forgiveness is and what it does and does not predict what the outcomes of forgiveness are likely to be
- Telling the story of the hurt in a supportive environment either through discussion, private reflection, or guided imagery is helpful
- Developing a sense of compassion and empathy for the transgressor by understanding her perspective and context issues which may have motivated her behavior can move a person toward forgiveness
- Admitting personal offenses helps victims identify with the transgressor role
- Making a conscious choice to forgive after comparing the pros and cons of forgiveness can be beneficial
- Letting go of residual negative emotions and inability to forgive can improve emotional and physical well-being

Konstam and colleagues (2003) view forgiveness as an empowering choice. They list the options for responding to hurt as retaliation, revenge, relinquishing, and reconciliation. When the victim has few options for the latter two, emotion focused coping can help them reframe and reappraise the offending event. They discuss the connection between a high degree of selfism (orientation to self) and unforgiveness.

In an interesting application of these concepts, Zechmeister & Romero (2002) explored forgiveness through narratives about unforgiveness and forgiveness. They believe there are two aspects to forgiveness: the inner emotional perspective and the social or behavioral perspective. One can change without the other. Operating on the premise that the objective truth is not as important as creation of a narrative that help make sense of a person's life story, these researchers had young adults write stories about situations where they hurt others, and then, in turn, create other narratives where they were on the receiving end of hurt. An analysis revealed that some victims were able to "end" their grudge through writing while others may have forgiven but they did not let go of the emotions connected to the grudge. Being able to empathize with the offender was an important correlate of forgiveness.

Exline and her research team (2004) looked at the quality of "narcissistic entitlement," believing that individuals with this trait would be less likely to forgive. Six linked studies explored their thesis in depth, confirming "narcissistic entitlement as a consistent, conceptually meaningful, and distinct predictor of unforgiveness. Entitled narcissists are readily offended, and they are eager to save face and defend their rights." (p.908). These researchers suggest an approach to promote forgiveness that helps the involved parties to examine what you owe others, and what they owe you, as well as the notion of "interpersonal debts."

Spiers (2004) looks at forgiveness as a crime prevention strategy, suggesting that forgiveness is not condoning, excusing, forgetting, or reconciling hurtful behaviors. His conclusion is that physical well-being is effected by the ability to forgive or not. Worthington & Scherer (2004) concur, noting that failure to forgive precipitates a stress response. The response may be delayed and compounded by an "injustice gap" which is the difference between a hoped for best possible resolution and the reality of the situation. Options for forgiving include restoring justice, perhaps through legal avenues, creating a new story about the grudge, perhaps through reframing or reworking the details, choosing to accept the situation and move on, becoming defensive and denying the reality of the situation, or forgiving. They believe: 1. failure to forgive is physically and emotionally stressful, 2. there is opportunity to move toward forgiveness, 3. forgiveness can undo some of the stress of unforgiveness, and 4. forgiveness can be a coping strategy which improves health.

Family Group Conferencing, an intervention mostly used in the juvenile justice system, is another strategy that can be utilized to help girls work out grudges. Blazemore & Umbreit (2001) describe this process and give an application example.

The process involves gathering a group of people most impacted by the grudge, including the begrudger, the begrudged and family and friends of both. Through a dialogue facilitated by a trained negotiator, the begrudged and her family talk about how she and others have been affected by the grudge, and what they believe can be done to resolve the issue. The process is then repeated by the begrudger and others in her sphere of family and friends. This allows the all parties to see the human impact that grudges can yield. All participants are encouraged to participate in brainstorming possible solutions to the problem and the sessions usually end with participants signing an agreement that details the specific actions that will lead to complete resolution.

Intervention Strategies

Resolving grudges is rarely a straightforward or simple task given the very nature of the situation. Motivating both parties to do the hard work of letting go of a grudge can be impossible, ruling out many of the ideal intervention options we traditionally pursue. Based on the literature reviewed for this book and our own experiences with girls, we offer the following steps as strategies which alone or in combination can be useful to one or more individuals involved in a grudge.

I. Prepare to Repair

■ **Assess how motivated those involved are to resolve the grudge:**

If one party is willing to reach out but the other refuses to engage, your approach will obviously have to focus more on one or more girl forgiving without condoning, and finding ways to live out the future knowing the grudge has not been completely resolved.

■ **Determine who is involved in the healing process:**

Although only one party involved in the grudge may come to you seeking help with resolution, all girls who are aware of the grudge are affected by it. The bystanders or witnesses who see the negative scenario play out day after day are also negatively impacted by the behaviors, even if they aren't directly involved. In some circumstances, you may even seek out the bystanders and enlist their help in budging the grudge.

■ **Understand the root of the behavior:**

It's not realistic to expect to persuade, threaten, bribe, or coerce someone into surrendering a grudge. Getting to the source of the negative feelings, and teasing out the emotional dynamics at work inside the begrudger, the begrudged, and all those girls around them who may fan the flames of negativity is an important first step. Layer by layer, you must explore the history of the grudge and it's present day outcomes, being careful to avoid blaming or condoning behaviors.

THE STORY

Girls need to tell their stories, whether they are the begruder or the begrudged. A question to ask to get at the heart of the matter (and we literally mean heart) is simply, "Tell me how things got to be this way with you and ____." (Avoid "why" or yes/no questions that shut down conversation, and don't call it a "grudge" to avoid negative connotations). It's important to really listen: commit to hearing her out until she finishes, don't interrupt, face her, allow enough time, and clarify details. Be aware of your own body language, facial expressions, and tone of voice.

2. Set to Get

What does everyone want? Once the preparation phase is completed, determine three things girls would like to see happen, in order of priority. Whether their goals are realistic or not, give them positive reinforcement for taking the step to identify them. For instance, if neither party wants to give up the grudge, what are the consequences of that choice likely to be?

For legal, medical, or ethical reasons, sometimes "no change" is not an option, so girls must turn to their second option. For example, if any girl or adult is close to an emotional or physical breakdown because of the grudge, continuing on "as is" won't be a viable option. At the same time, having a goal of resolving the grudge by tomorrow is probably not likely to happen—although never rule out the unpredictable!

Some realistic goals might be:
- Have both parties tell their stories and share them
- Develop some positive strategies to cope with negative behaviors
- Eliminate overt hostility
- Have a one week moratorium on the grudge

3. Choose to Lose

Give it up: Regardless of the goals, girls must recognize they need to let go of something in order to move forward in budging their grudge. What is given up may range from one day of hostility to a complete surrender, but being honest about what is and is not possible is important.

Feel for her: One way to move toward mutual forgiveness is to develop a sense of similarity between girls involved in the grudge, and developing a bigger perspective of relationship skills. While it's true that in this situation, one girl has launched the grudge, in other situations, she may have been on the receiving end, as is true for all parties involved. Taking a look backward at other times and places when the grudge roles could have easily been switched is one way for girls to recognize that they are capable giving or receiving hurtful behavior in what is often equal measure.

Letting go: Releasing negative behaviors can only be done by the parties involved in a grudge. Making a conscious choice to be done with the grudge, whether or not the feeling is mutual, is a hard choice—but it is a choice. Understanding that releasing the behavior does not mean agreeing that the other party is wrong or right, or even forgiving her.

Forgiveness: Going the next step to truly forgive their offenders is a challenge to many girls. Some useful questions might be:
- When you think about this situation, what one word comes to mind?
- What do you think it would take to repair the situation between you and _____?
- If it's not "fixable" how can you coexist?

Have a toolkit of strategies: Developing a Plan A, B, C for the future will help empower girls to follow through with action steps to resolve the grudge. Rehearsing, and asking "What will this look like when you're together?" as well as role playing can be beneficial.

4. Endure for More

Persist: Stress the importance of perseverance. The longer the grudge has been held, the longer it will take to resolve it. Helping girls stay on track with shifting negative dynamics will not only address the situation at hand but teach an important life skill. Encourage them not to give up, even when obstacles arise.

Follow up: Continue to work with girls even though this particular grudge may be resolved. Ongoing contact will not only show your concern, but increases the likelihood that the changes will continue, rather than a lapse back into destructive interaction styles.

5. Faith Perspectives

Most faith traditions embrace forgiveness, rather than grudge holding. Mohammed Abu-Nimer says: "Forgiveness as a way of healing human relationships and solving human conflicts is an age-old practice that appears in numerous religious traditions across the globe, (2001). Said & Funk (2001) say: "…religion profoundly influences goal-seeking behavior in conflict situations, by establishing the criteria or frames of reference for determining the rightness and wrongness of events." Many religious texts such as the Bible, the Torah, the Quran, or the Vedas, to name a few, can be valuable resources that offer wisdom on releasing or resolving grudges.

This faith perspective often helps girls view the grudge from a more altruistic standpoint, helping her to understand that holding grudges and unforgiveness is a detriment to not only her physical but spiritual self. The power of forgiveness, rather than perceived justice, can be a pathway to peace for all involved.

Interventions to Integrate Change

Activity #16:
Action Plan to Resolve a Grudge

Objectives:
Upon completion of this activity, girls will:
- Create a plan for resolving a grudge
- Discuss the feasibility of the plan
- Develop action steps to implement the plan

Procedure:
Sometimes, when emotions are heated and it seems there is no way to resolve a grudge, writing things out in an Action Plan can be helpful. Note this is a plan, and as such each girl has the option of doing nothing more than creating it. The process of creation, though, can be a helpful jumpstart to action.

Using the *My Action Plan worksheet*, determine how motivated a girl is to carry it out. It is okay not to be a "10!" Even a 1 is better than zero. Ask what it would take to move the girl higher on the scale, and revisit to determine if the score changes, or any of the action steps need revised.

My Action Plan

My goal is to:_____

What will help me achieve this goal?_____

_____

What might make it difficult?_____

_____

Who is involved in my plan?_____

_____

How many days/weeks/months will is take to complete this plan?_____

List the steps, in order, needed to carry out this plan:

1._____

2._____

3._____

4._____

My motivation to start this plan is:

1------2------3------4------5------6--------7------8------9------10
Not at all   Motivated   As motivated
motivated   as possible

Interventions to Integrate Change

Activity #17:
No Grudge Goal Book

Objectives:
Upon completion of this activity, girls will:
- Track changes in grudge behaviors over time
- Empower girls to identify choices around grudge behaviors
- Write about the connection between grudge related feelings and behaviors

Procedure:
Setting goals and keeping a record can be a powerful way to keep grudge resolutions on a girl's radar screen from day to day. You can either purchase a journal, provide a copy of the *My Grudge Goal Book* worksheet, or give copies of the actual template with a folder with pockets to keep them in. Privacy is important, so you may decide to keep the folder or journal and give it to the girl as needed. She may write once a week, daily, or as often as needed.

Discuss her writing each time she sets a goal and see what progress she is or isn't making in achieving her goal. If she doesn't seem to be moving forward, is the goal realistic? Talk about the choices she is making in relation to grudge behaviors, and which are going to help achieve her goal. Finally, dialogue about the relationship between how she feels and how she acts in a grudge situation.

My Grudge Goal Book

Date:_____

My grudge goal for the upcoming day/week/month is to: _____

_____

Some examples of the grudge behaviors that need to change include:

_____

_____

Some substitute behaviors I can think of are: _____

_____

_____

Since I last wrote, my feelings about the grudge are: _____

_____

_____

Since I last wrote, the grudge behaviors that were used by me or others include:

_____

_____

The connection I see between grudge feelings and grudge behaviors since I last wrote is:_____

_____

Interventions to Integrate Change

Activity #18:
Grudge Guru

Objectives:
Upon completion of this activity, girls will:
- Promote a dialogue about grudges between girls
- Identify common themes around girl grudges
- Use wisdom of other girls to promote insight into personal grudges
- Practice positive communication skills

Procedure:
This activity will help girls engage in conversation around the topic of grudges, thereby enhancing communication skills. It can be done as a group activity, or as an individual. The assignment is to interview as many other girls as possible about their experiences with grudges.

Provide the girls copies of the *Be A Grudge Guru Interview Questions* worksheet, and plenty of paper to write on. Stress that no real names or identifying details are to be used in the writing (i.e. someone is the captain of the girls swim team, plays trumpet in the band, has frizzy red hair, etc.).

If doing this activity as a group, have girls count off by two's and then pair them up with someone they don't know. Try to have them switch partners as many times as possible, and then switch roles so the person interviewed gets to be the interviewer.

If doing this activity as an individual, have girls interview as many other women as possible as a "homework assignment," using the questions worksheet. Stress that the women they interview need not be students at the same school or even the same age: relatives, neighbors, and others are fine.

Be A Grudge Guru Interview Questions

What do you consider to be a grudge? _____

_____

_____

Can you tell me about a grudge you were involved in? _____

_____

_____

How did the grudge get resolved? _____

_____

_____

What do you wish had happened differently about the grudge? _____

_____

_____

What advice would you give girls about grudges? _____

_____

_____

Interventions to Integrate Change

Activity #19:
A Letter to Myself

Objectives:
Upon completion of this activity, girls will:
- Gain insight about personal grudges
- Put their thoughts in writing for future reference
- Use time as a resource for developing a different perspective about a grudge

Procedure:
Writing a letter to oneself can be an effective way to explore emotions around a particular issue. Begin by having girls write a letter as if to a friend, describing the grudge and what has happened as a result of it. Stop and discuss what has been written, then instruct them to go on and write about what they wish would happen in the future. Set a specific timeline, i.e. "By next month I wish that….."

Now have girls take another piece of paper and write an identical letter, only from the point of view of the person who opposes them in a grudge. Describe her perceptions of what has happened, and discuss this. Continue to write about what they think the other girl would like to happen in the future, again setting a specific timeline: "By next month, I wish that……"

Compare similarities and differences in the letters, then seal both in an envelope and reopen when the date on the timeline arrives. See how close to reality the letters seem, given the benefit of time.

Interventions to Integrate Change

Activity #20:
Emotion Lotion

Objectives:
Upon completion of this activity, girls will:
- Identify emotions which may lead to destructive behaviors
- Explore alternative coping strategies
- Create a plan for dealing with a grudge that uses at least one healthy coping strategy

Procedure:
In the midst of a grudge, negative emotions can often give rise to destructive behaviors. Consider:
- *Months later, Ellie still explodes in rage each time she sees Rhiannon, the girl who stole her ex-boyfriend in seventh grade.*

- *Ismee hides in the bathroom each time she sees Lana, a girl who has hated her ever since her family moved out of the neighborhood where they both lived many years ago.*

- *Maritza keeps all of her girlfriends alienated from Luze, who used to be part of their crowd, because their sisters had a huge fight and are no longer friends.*

Anger and fear are two of the biggest emotions that fuel grudges—although many others fan the flames and keep the conflict going. Hand out three index cards to each girl, and have her list one emotion on each that she feels when she is involved in the grudge. No names should be used.

When the cards are completed, collect them, shuffle the cards, and begin by reading the emotion word written on the top card. Ask for all girls to come up with some helpful strategies that will help address this difficult emotion. (Avoid labeling behaviors as "good" or "bad.")

Suggestions from real girls for dealing with angry emotions:
- Take a few deep breaths before responding
- Walk away to compose yourself
- Count to ten before saying anything
- Sing a calming song inside your head
- Talk things out with an adult who can help
- Ask yourself: "Is it worth getting upset over this?"
- Consider the consequences

Alternatives for fearful emotions include:
- Have a safe place and a safe person at all times
- Learn to express yourself in ways that won't make the situation worse
- Stand by others
- Use positive self talk ("I am not afraid")
- Pray
- Write in a journal
- Learn martial arts to build your confidence (not to threaten someone!)

Interventions to Integrate Change

Activity #21:
Act It Out

Objectives:
Upon completion of this activity, girls will:
- Use drama to gain insight into the dynamics of grudges
- Express their emotional response to grudges
- Rehearse alternative behaviors which can be used by those involved in a grudge

Procedure:
Begin by writing a play about the grudge, which is different than writing the story of a grudge. Select one "scene" from the grudge and pretend you are a screenwriter about to create a movie out of that particular situation. You can use this example to get started, or, if girls don't want to write about and act out their own situations, they can use this one.

● ●

THE GRUDGE GIRLS

The setting is a crowded hallway in a small rural middle school. It's the end of the day, and kids are everywhere, trying to get to their lockers so they can catch the bus or walk home.

At the end of the hallway, Sandee, a small, attractive girl, is surrounded by two other girls, who are talking nonstop and trying to get her attention. As Sandee takes her books out of the locker, she notices Llenae, an equally attractive girl, coming down the hall from the opposite direction. Sandee and Llenae used to be best friends until last summer, when Llenae made fun of Sandee's bathing suit in front of a crowd of guys at the swimming pool. Ever since then, they have been part of an ongoing "word war" that also uses hurtful behaviors to "one up" the other.

Sandee Friend One: "So Sandee, what's the plan for this weekend---"

Sandee Friend Two: (whining) "Sandee, you promised you were having a sleepover---"

Sandee (notices Llenae walking past): "Hey there, sticky fingers. Heard you got caught shoplifting at WalMart last night."

Llenae pauses and turns around as Sandee and her friends laugh.

Activity #21:
Act It Out (continued)

Sandee Friend One: "Yeah, didn't anyone ever tell you, friends don't let friends steal!"

Llenae: "I didn't steal anything, slut face. (She comes closer to Sandee.) I'm getting tired of you and your accusations."

Sandee: "Yeah, the truth hurts, doesn't it?" (Her friends laugh as Llenae pushes Sandee against her locker.)

Llenae: "I'll tell you what—if you don't shut that big mouth of yours, I'll do it for you."

Sandee: "Oh yeah?"

At this point, other students gather around the girls, chanting, "Fight! Fight! Fight!"
End here.

• •

"Interview" the characters in the drama to determine their motivation.
In the scenario above, you might ask:
- Why did Sandee's friends automatically side with her?
- What made Llenae make fun of Sandee last summer?
- Why is Sandee so angry with Llenae?
- What emotions might all of the girls involved in this scene be feeling?
- Now rewrite the drama using either the example above, or another one that has been created.

Interventions to Integrate Change

Activity #22:
Family Group Conferencing

Objectives:
Upon completion of this activity, girls will:
- Discuss the grudge with family and friends
- Explore alternatives for resolving the grudge
- Have a signed contract of strategies for all parties to use to resolve or release the grudge

Procedure:
Find a neutral spot to meet that has no emotional connotation for the girls or adults involved. This might be a conference room in a business building, a meeting room in a church or synagogue, or another location that is not normally part of the girls' world.

Set up the environment with adequate space and privacy. Either write out some guidelines on a poster ahead of time or create a handout that frames the session. These might include:
"We are here because all of us care about these young women. We respect that each person who has come to this meeting plays an important role in helping _____ and _____ look at ways to resolve some issues that are creating problems for both of them. We would ask that each of you take turns talking, and speak only for yourself, that is, use "I" kinds of statements. (Explain what I statements are.) We plan for this session to last about 90 minutes in order to let everyone have enough time to express themselves."

It's imperative to separately interview the begrudged and the begrudger ahead of time, and to have them create a narrative of what happened between them that led to this point. This avoids a lot of "she saids" which may distract from the conference. Have the stories then typed up so you can share them during the family conference.

Begin by reading the stories without identifying who wrote them. Stress that you are not presenting either one as the absolute truth or one as "right" and the other "wrong" but rather as the perceptions of the girls involved, which is what is most important.

Activity #22:
Family Group Conferencing *(continued)*

Ask for all of those in attendance to listen to each story without interruption. Once you are done, ask the following questions, making sure to solicit input from everyone in attendance by going around the room and asking:

1. When you heard these stories, tell me one or two words that came to mind.

2. Ask each person to describe in one sentence how the grudge/conflict has impacted on them.

3. What do you think it will take to help the girls involved in this situation move toward resolving the grudge. (Explain that you do not believe nor is it realistic to expect a magical and instant solution. Make a list of steps on the board or a tablet if possible.)

4. Ask the girls involved which of the steps they agree and disagree with, and which they think they might realistically use to resolve their conflict.

5. Create an action plan that all parties can agree with, and have everyone in attendance sign it.

The initial conference should be the beginning of a process which will lead to resolution of the grudge. Reconvene meetings as needed and have each person provide input on progress being made, continuing challenges, etc. Make sure to recognize girls for forward momentum which includes attending the meetings you have arranged!

Interventions to Integrate Change

Activity #23:
Divine Intervention

Objectives:
Upon completion of this activity, girls will:
- Use religious teachings as a resource for resolving grudges
- Explore alternative religious/spiritual perspectives for use as action strategies
- Discuss personal beliefs and values which influence attitudes and behavior.

Procedure:
Many faith traditions focus on forgiveness, and releasing grudges. See if girls can come up with some quotes from various religions that deal with forgiveness, grudges, or just relationships.

Distribute copies of the *Words of Wisdom* worksheet. (For girls from faith traditions not represented, an additional "Other:" section is provided.)

Explore the following questions:

1. Do any of these quotes say something meaningful to you about grudges?

2. Do you notice any differences or similarities between the quotes?

3. What helpful advice do you find in these quotes?

Have girls select one of the quotes and write about how they might use it to change their lives tomorrow. In other words, what is one bit of "take home" advice that has application for real life?

Challenge them to find other quotes in religious texts that might help approach forgiveness and grudges from a different perspective. Compile a list and suggest that girls read over them in the morning as they prepare to go about their day.

Words of Wisdom

Leviticus 19:17-18:
Thou shalt not hate thy brother in thine heart: thou shalt in any wise rebuke thy neighbour, and not suffer sin upon him. Thou shalt not avenge, nor bear any grudge against the children of thy people, but thou shalt love thy neighbour as thyself: I am the LORD.'

Colossians 3:12-14:
Therefore, as God's chosen people, holy and dearly loved, clothe yourselves with compassion, kindness, humility, gentleness and patience. [13] Bear with each other and forgive whatever grievances you may have against one another. Forgive as the Lord forgave you. [14] And over all these virtues put on love, which binds them all together in perfect unity.

Luke 23:33-34:
When they came to the place called the Skull, there they crucified him, along with the criminals--one on his right, the other on his left. [34] Jesus said, "Father, forgive them, for they do not know what they are doing." And they divided up his clothes by casting lots.

Mark 11:25:
And when you stand praying, if you hold anything against anyone, forgive him, so that your Father in heaven may forgive you your sins."

Islam (Shiite).
Nahjul Balagha, Saying 201:
The best deed of a great man is to forgive and forget.

Islam. Qur'an 64.14:
If you efface and overlook and forgive, then lo! God is forgiving, merciful.

Islam. Hadith of Baihaqi:
Moses son of Imran said, "My Lord, who is the greatest of Thy servants in Thy estimation?" and received the reply, "The one who forgives when he is in a position of power."

Islam. Qur'an 42.36-43:
Better and more rewarding is God's reward to those who believe and put their trust in Him: who avoid gross sins and indecencies and, when angered, are willing to forgive... Let evil be rewarded by like evil, but he who forgives and seeks reconciliation shall be rewarded by God. He does not love the wrongdoers.... True constancy lies in forgiveness and patient forbearance.

Taoism. Tao Te Ching 79:
In reconciling a great injury,
Some injury is sure to remain.
How can this be good?
Therefore the sage holds the left-hand tally [obligation] of a contract;
He does not blame others.
The person of virtue attends to the obligation; The person without virtue attends to the exactions.

Confucianism. I Ching 40: Release:
The superior man tends to forgive wrongs and deals leniently with crimes.

Other:

Interventions to Integrate Change

Activity #24:
Word Search

Objectives:
Upon completion of this activity, girls will:
- Demonstrate a comprehensive understanding of words connected to grudges
- Use a word search activity to stimulate discussion about grudges
- Identify words which represent behaviors they do and do not want to use in the future

Procedure:
After completing the *Grudge Word Search* worksheet, check the Key below for answers. Discuss each of the search words and how they might relate to grudges. Then challenge girls to identify the opposite of each word listed, and choose those that represent behaviors they wish to use in future interactions.

Grudge Words Key

Argument	Humiliate
Bitter	Hurt
Clash	Individual
Competition	Institutional
Conflict	Jealousy
Disagreement	Judgment
Deep	Misunderstood
Dislike	Offend
Dispute	Ongoing
Enduring	Quarrel
Fight	Resent
Gossip	Rivalry
Harm	Sabotage
Hate	Snub
Hidden	Tension

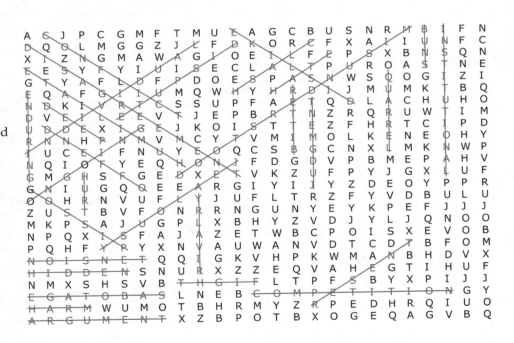

Grudge Word Search

Find as many words as you can that relate to a grudge.

```
A C J P C G M F T M U E E A G C B U S N R M B I F N
D Q O L M G G Z J L F D K O R C F X A I I A U N F C
X I Z N G G M A I I I I E L I L F E S R X B N S Q N
E E S Y F F Y L D U F R E S Y A T P N Q R O Q G F E
G T Q A G Y I I T C U M S F F A R D T I Z M A K Z I
E Q A F G V R E V U S S Y B P H R T N Z U W Q U H Q
N D K I I R I T E J T J C F B S E T E M Z D R C W O
D V E V L E M G V M Y M O I T V T I M Z O F N R U M
U D D I X P N V M Y E O N Q C I T B G C R L K N M D
R N U C E I F M N E O X O E Y V S D G D V L X M E Y
I Q C G O F Y E Q Y H X A R O J C F Z U P X B Y G P
N M I O H S F G O D E A Y H G F D K I J Y P Y J X V
G O G H S G Q V O E E L N R J V K I T R Z F B E O F
O U H R N B V F O F N R X R G I L Y N Z E Y D V X R
Z S R S B V U F G A J P L A U G F U Z V D K P E Y U
M K P A I J U G A X N P R X B H T W B J I L S P B J
N P Q X I Y S P U F Y T E B E T W A H N C D X E B O
P Q H F Y N P E Y T S N Q I R K V M H P I S N T B B
H O I S S N E N B Q U Q R X G B V K Z I C D B H M X
N I D D E H O V A A M R N B H B P K Z Q A E G T X F
E M X S T O W V M S O T B B E U A V F A E B B I I J
H A R T M H W B Z H L C M Y Z X P R E D E H R Q U O
A R G U M E N T X Z B P O T B R O G E Q A G V B Q
```

Argument	Bitter	Clash	Competition
Conflict	Disagreement	Deep	Dislike
Dispute	Enduring	Fight	Gossip
Harm	Hate	Hidden	Humiliate
Hurt	Individual	Institutional	Jealousy
Judgment	Misunderstood	Offend	Ongoing
Quarrel	Resent	Rivalry	Sabotage
Snub	Tension		

67

Interventions to Integrate Change

Activity #25:
A Grudge Cross Word Puzzle

Objectives:
Upon completion of this activity, girls will:
- Evaluate their understanding of grudges
- Use new information to create personal change strategies
- Define key behaviors of girls involved in grudges, and possible strategies to address them.

Procedure:
Complete the crossword puzzle on the next page, and then consult the Key below for answers. Discuss the words and their definitions to see if there is additional information that should or could be added.

Ask girls to identify a personal solution they might use to address each of the grudge behaviors on the puzzle in a positive way. Make a list of the ones which can be used "Immediately," "Within One Week," and "Within One Month." Encourage girls to keep track of their progress in implementing these new behaviors.

Crossword Puzzle Answer Key

Across

5. Argument
7. Hate
10. Bitter
11. Ongoing
12. Dispute
13. Tension
16. Snub
17. Hidden
18. Gossip
19. Quarrel
20. Misunderstood

Down

1. Harm
2. Conflict
3. Rivalry
4. Hurt
6. Jealousy
8. Fight
9. Judgment
14. Offend
15. Humiliate

A Grudge Crossword Puzzle

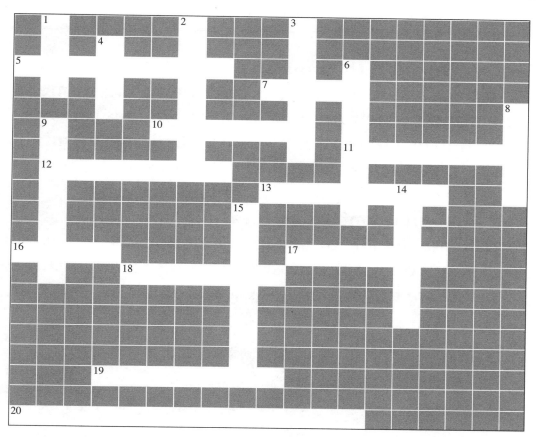

ACROSS

5. A heated verbal disagreement
7. Intense Dislike
10. When we hold ill feelings towards others we are said to be _____ towards them.
11. Something that continues for a long time.
12. A verbal disagreement
13. Fighting and aggression creates _____ and stress between friends.
16. To exclude or ignore someone
17. Unable to see
18. Spreading rumors about others is known as _____.
19. A fight between two individuals
20. When you do something that is taken the wrong way you are said to be _____.

DOWN

1. To hurt someone physically or verbally
2. A quarrel or ongoing disagreement between two individuals
3. Competition between two individuals creates _____.
4. Relational Aggression will cause you to feel ____.
6. Envying something or someone else
8. A physical or verbal altercation
9. To create an opinion about someone or something
14. To do or say something inappropriate may _____ someone, causing mental hurt.
15. When someone extremely embarrasses you they _____ you.

SUMMARY

"We hope the information in this book
will be of value to both you and the young women
you are shaping for the future. Although grudges can seem to be
the ultimate and most impossible challenge an adult
can face when guiding girls, the time and effort
we spend doing so is among our most
important missions. Learning to resolve
conflict and "let go" of negative emotions is a valuable
life skill—and one of the most rewarding accomplishments
we can achieve—or teach others."

REFERENCES

Abu-Nimer, M. (Ed.). (2001). *Reconciliation, Coexistence, and Justice in Interethnic Conflicts: Theory and Practice.* Lanham, MD: Lexington Books.

Bazemore, G., & Umbreit, M. (2001). *Family group conferencing.* (Juvenile Justice Bulletin). Washington, D.C.: Office of Juvenile Justice and Delinquency Prevention. Retrieved on May 11, 2007 from http://www.ncjrs.gov/html/ojjdp/2001_2_1/page3.html

Burgess, H., & Burgess, G. (November, 2003). *What are intractable conflicts? Beyond Intractability: A Free Knowledge Base on More Constructive Approaches to Destructive Conflict.* Retrieved April 27, 2007, from http://www.beyondintractability.org/essay/meaning_intractability/?nid=1003

Burton, V. (September 13, 2005). *Let go of your grudges.* Ask Volrie: Black America Web. Retrieved April 27, 2007 from http://www.blackamericaweb.com/site.aspx/Praise/challenge/grudges91305 http://medjournal.hmc.psu.edu:2062/gw1/ovidweb.cgi?S=IDNJHKKOJHMBJM00D&Search+Link=%22Exline%2c+Julie+Juola%22.au

Exline, J., Baumeister, R., Bushman, B., Campbell W., & Finkel, E. (2004). *Too proud to let go: Narcissistic entitlement as a barrier to forgiveness.* Journal of Personality and Social Psychology. 87, 894-912.

Harrison, L. (2006). *The Clique: Complete Set of 6 Paperbacks.* New York: Simon& Schuster.

Jameson, J. The escalation and de-escalation of intractable conflict.. Paper presented Thursday, October 4, 2001 in the Caldwell Lounge at NC State University. Retrieved April 27, 2007 from http://www.ncsu.edu/chass/communication/www/alumnicircle/cwt/jameson.htm

Jenkins, R. (Producer). (2003). *America's next top model.* [Television series]. United States: UPN Television.

Juan, A., & Chang, W. (Producers) (2005). *My super sweet 16.* United States: MTV Networks.

Karremans, J., Van Lange, P., & Holland, R. (2005). *Forgiveness and its associations with prosocial thinking, feeling, and doing beyond the relationship with the offender.* Personality and Social Psychology Bulletin, 31, 1315.

Konstam, V., Holmes, W., & Levine, B. (2003). *Empathy, selfism, and coping as elements of the psychology of forgiveness: A preliminary study.* Counseling and Values, 47, 172.

Maslow, A. (1954). *Motivation and personality.* New York: Harper.

Maslow, A. (1971). *The farther reaches of human nature.* New York: The Viking Press.

Maslow, A., & Lowery, R. (Eds.). (1998). Toward a psychology of being (3rd ed.). New York: Wiley & Sons.

Merriam-Webster Dictionary. (2005). Springfield, MA: Merriam-Webster.

REFERENCES (continued)

Northrup, T. (1989). "The dynamic of identity in personal and social conflict." In L. Kriesberg, T.A. Northrup, and S.J. Thorson (eds.), Intractable conflicts and their transformation. Syracuse, NY: Syracuse University Press.

Random House Webster's Unabridged Dictionary, Second Edition (2005) New York: www.amazon.com/exec/obidos/search-handle-url/104-5527973-7363129?%5Fencoding=UTF8&search-type=ss&index=books&field-author=Random%20House" Random House

Reed, P. (Producer), & Bendinger, J. (Writer). (2000). *Bring it on* [Motion picture]. United States: Beacon Communications.

Said, A., & Funk, N. (2001). The role of faith in cross-cultural conflict resolution. Paper presented at the European Parliament for the European Centre for Common Ground, September 2001.

Spiers, A. (2004). Forgiveness as a secondary prevention strategy for victims of interpersonal crime. Australasian Psychiatry, 12 261-263.

Tennen, M. (2006). *Letting go of grudges. Health AtoZ: A world of health at your fingertips.* Retrieved April 27, 2007 from www.healthatoz.com

VanOyen Witvliet C., Ludwig, T., & Vander Laan, K.. (2001). *Granting forgiveness or harboring grudges: Implications for emotion, physiology, and health.* Psychological Science, 12 117-123.

Wade, N., & Worthington, E. (2003). *Overcoming interpersonal offenses: Is forgiveness the only way to deal with unforgiveness?* Journal of Counseling & Development, 81343-353.

Worthington, E., Mazzeo, S., Kliewer, & Wendy L. (2002). *Addictive and eating disorders, unforgiveness, and forgiveness.* Journal of Psychology and Christianity, 21 257-261.

Worthington, E. & Scherer, M. (2004). Forgiveness is an emotion-focused coping strategy that can reduce health risks and promote health resilience: Theory, review, and hypotheses. Psychology & Health, 19 385-405.

Zechmeister, J. & Romero, C. (2002). Victim and offender accounts of interpersonal conflict: Autobiographical narratives of forgiveness and unforgiveness. Journal of Personality and Social Psychology, . 82 675-686.

Ziegesar, C. (2003). *Gossip Girl Boxed Set.* New York: Megan Tingley Books.

WEBSITES

Center for Media Literacy
The Center for Media Literacy (CML) is a nonprofit educational organization that provides leadership, public education, professional development and educational resources nationally. Dedicated to promoting and supporting media literacy education as a framework for accessing, analyzing, evaluating and creating media content, CML works to help citizens, especially the young, develop critical thinking and media production skills needed to live fully in the 21st century media culture. The ultimate goal is to make wise choices possible.
www.medialit.org

Club and Camp Ophelia
Club and Camp Ophelia use a unique and creative framework to help girls learn positive relationship skills. Officially, it's called ERI (educate, relate, integrate), but girls refer to it as just plain fun. Again and again, the opportunity to make new friends and enjoy a safe "girls only" environment are what girls say they like most about both programs.
www.clubophelia.com

Conflict Research Consortium at the University of Colorado
The Conflict Research Consortium is a multi-disciplinary center for research and teaching about conflict and its transformation. The primary focus is difficult and intractable conflicts.
http://conflict.colorado.edu/

Courage for Youth
Courage for Youth is proactive and solution-oriented. Our desire is to strengthen young peoples' self-esteem, to prevent relational aggression, and to thwart suicide, depression, eating disorders, poor self image, loneliness, and poisonous media influence. Prevention is far more cost effective than intervention!
www.courageforyouth.com

Getting Along in School
This website offers girls an opportunity to share their experiences and offer tips for stronger friendships.
www.timeforkids.com/TFK/magazines/story/0,6277,234781,00.html

Girls, Inc.
Girls Incorporated is a national nonprofit youth organization dedicated to inspiring all girls to be strong, smart, and bold. With roots dating to 1864, Girls Inc has provided vital educational programs to millions of American girls, particularly those in high-risk, underserved areas. Today, innovative programs help girls confront subtle societal messages about their value and potential, and prepare them to lead successful, independent, and fulfilling lives.
www.girlsinc.org

Girl Power!
The national public education campaign sponsored by the U.S. Department of Health and Human Services to help encourage and motivate 9- to 13- year-old girls to make the most of their lives. Girls at 8 or 9 typically have very strong attitudes about their health, so Girl Power! seeks to reinforce and sustain these positive values among girls ages 9-13 by targeting health messages to the unique needs, interests, and challenges of girls.
www.girlpower.gov

Managing Student Behavior in Today's Schools
This multiple research initiative studies conflict resolution and peer mediation in middle schools and the preventive effects of an anger management/social problem solving curriculum for K-12 students.
http://education.ufl.edu/web/?pid=305

National Institute on Media and the Family:
The National Institute on Media and the Family has works to help parents and communities "watch what our kids watch." The National Institute on Media and the Family is one of the world's leading and most respected research-based organization on the positive and harmful effects of media on children and youth.
http://www.mediaandthefamily.org

National Parenting Center:
The National Parenting Center provides one of the most comprehensive and responsible parenting advice to parents everywhere. The advice provided is furnished by some of the world's most respected authorities in the field of child rearing and development.
www.tnpc.com

Parenting Today's Teen:
Parenting Today's Teen provides information and articles organized by topics, such as, Teen Health; Education; Troubled Teens; Teen Drug Abuse; Tips For Parenting Teens; and Other Teen Issues.   All of the articles featured on this site have been written by parents that have gained experience by raising teens of their own.
www.parentingteens.com

Positive Parenting Online:
Positive Parenting is dedicated to providing resources and information to help make parenting more rewarding, effective and fun.
www.positiveparenting.com

The Ophelia Project
The Ophelia Project raises awareness about relational aggression, provides educational resources and original programs and advocates for healthy peer relationships.
www.opheliaproject.org

Tolerance.org
Tolerance.org is a principal online destination for people interested in dismantling bigotry and creating, in hate's stead, communities that value diversity. If you want to know how to transform yourself, your home, your school, your workplace or your community, Tolerance.org is a place to start — and continue — the journey. Through its online well of resources and ideas, its expanding collection of print materials, its burgeoning outreach efforts, and its downloadable public service announcements, Tolerance.org promotes and supports anti-bias activism in every venue of life.
www.tolerance.org

WEB ARTICLES

Girl Violence and Aggression: Problems and Solutions
This report explores whether or why girl violence is on the rise, the causes of such real or perceived increase in violent behavior, and what needs to be done to address the problem.
http://www.co.cook.il.us/Agencies/wc/cc_wc_girls_violence_Aug2006.pdf

Letting Go of Grudges
This article provides practical tips on how to let go of grudges
www.healthatoz.com

Let Go of Your Grudges
This article explores the affects that grudges have on your health and provides strategies to help resolve grudges in a healthy way.
www.blackamericaweb.com

Don't Hold a Grudge
This article focuses on why people have grudges, what grudges do to the them and how to let go.
www.cope-inc.com/grudge.html

Countering Gender Bias in the Media
This article explores the issues of gender equity and bias in the media
www.nsta.org/main/news/pdf/ss0203_40.pdf

At the time of this publishing date, all the websites were reviewed at the URL listed. The content at that time was as described in the websites listed, and the access information correct. Some of these websites may have changed since the publishing of this book.